TOUCH AND THE HEALING OF THE WORLD

Touch

and the

Healing of the World

Daniel B. Hinshaw

ST VLADIMIR'S SEMINARY PRESS
YONKERS, NEW YORK
2017

Library of Congress Cataloging-in-Publication Data

Library of Congress Cataloging-in-Publication Data
Names: Hinshaw, Daniel B., author. Title: Touch and the healing of the world /
    Daniel B. Hinshaw.
Description: Yonkers, NY : St Vladimir's Seminary Press, 2017. | Description
    based on print version record and CIP data provided by publisher; resource not
    viewed.
Identifiers: LCCN 2017023531 (print) | LCCN 2017025347 (ebook) | ISBN
    9780881416008 | ISBN 9780881415995
Subjects: LCSH: Healing—Religious aspects—Orthodox Eastern Church. |
    Orthodox Eastern Church—Doctrines.
Classification: LCC BX323 (ebook) | LCC BX323 .H567 2017 (print) | DDC
    234/.131—dc23
LC record available at https://lccn.loc.gov/2017023531

Copyright © 2017

ST VLADIMIR'S SEMINARY PRESS
575 Scarsdale Road
Yonkers, New York 10707
1–800–204–2665
www.svspress.com

ISBN 978–0–88141–599–5 (print)
ISBN 978–0–88141–600–8 (electronic)

Printed in the United States of America

That unreachable power came down and put on limbs that could be touched so that the needy could approach Him and, embracing His humanity, become aware of His divinity.*

—St Ephrem the Syrian (+373), *Homily on Our Lord*

*St Ephrem the Syrian (+373), *Homily on Our Lord* 10.2, trans. Edward G. Mathews and Joseph P. Amar, in *Healing in the Theology of Saint Ephrem*, by Aho Shemunkasho (Piscataway, NJ: Gorgias Press, 2004), 229.

Table of Contents

Dedication

THIS BOOK IS DEDICATED to the memory of Fr Roman Braga (+2015), one of the defenders and confessors of the faith, who suffered during the extreme travail imposed upon Romania by the Communists. Since His Beatitude Daniel, patriarch of the Orthodox Church of Romania, has declared 2017 to be the Commemorative Year of the Defenders of Orthodoxy during Communism,[1] this is an auspicious time to publish this small volume in honor of Fr Roman. Through the great mercy and economy of God, after suffering eleven years of imprisonment—including the horrors of Stalin's experimental attempt to create a "Communist personality" at Pitesti, extended solitary confinement, hard labor in the Danube Delta, and house arrest—Fr Roman was exiled from his native country, first to Brazil and eventually to the United States of America.[2] Ironically, the Communist regime in Romania, in ridding itself of this "troublesome" priest, set in motion his apostolic mission to the Western Hemisphere, for which those who have been blessed to know him are deeply grateful.

To my great joy, I discovered in Fr Roman a mentor and spiritual father who could teach me about the mystery of healing that is so intimately connected with suffering—a mystery that he had learned not from theoretical knowledge, but from his direct experience. Along with others, it was my great privilege to assist in the care of Fr Roman during his slow decline over the last two years of his life. It was during this

---

[1] *Aurelian Iftimiu,* "Solemn and Commemorative Year 2017 officially proclaimed in the Romanian Patriarchate," News Agency Basilica.ro, January 3, 2017, accessed April 30, 2017, *http://basilica.ro/en/solemn-and-commemorative-year-2017-officially-proclaimed-in-the-romanian-patriarchate/.*

[2] J. M. Kushiner, "Solitary Refinement: How One Man Found Freedom Inside a Communist Prison; An Interview with Fr. Roman Braga," accessed April 26, 2017, *http://www.salvomag.com/new/articles/salvo26/solitary-refinement.php.*

period that this book project, in collaboration with Holy Dormition Monastery, was conceived and initiated with his blessing. He was particularly interested in seeing the combination of iconography with a written exploration of the sense of touch and its relationship to healing within the Tradition of the Church. My hope and prayer is that in some small way, this book approaches the clarity of vision and joy of living continually in the presence of Christ that Fr Roman typified.

May his memory be eternal!

Plate 1

Introduction

Now Moses was keeping the flock of his father-in-law, Jethro, the priest of Midian; and he led his flock to the west side of the wilderness, and came to Horeb, the mountain of God. And the angel of the Lord appeared to him in a flame of fire out of the midst of a bush; and he looked, and lo, the bush was burning, yet it was not consumed. And Moses said, "I will turn aside and see this great sight, why the bush is not burnt." When the Lord saw that he turned aside to see, God called to him out of the bush, "Moses, Moses!" And he said, "Here am I." Then he said, "Do not come near; put off your shoes from your feet, for the place on which you are standing is holy ground."

—Ex 3.1–5 (RSV)

TOUCH, THAT MOST BASIC, most humble of the senses, is at the heart of the contact between God and his creature. Implicit within matter, the very substance of the created order, is the possibility of contact. In reality, all of the senses—sight, hearing, smell, and taste—are derivative of the sense of touch, a principle understood as early as the fifth century BC by the ancient Greek philosopher Democritus in his speculations concerning the atomic nature of matter.[1] Even the other senses depend on some form of contact: photons of light with sensors in the eye, the pressure exerted by sound waves on the eardrum, and molecules binding to receptors in transducing the senses of smell and taste. God touches us through time and space. From the moment of creation, the dance of time, energy, and matter began. We still receive visions of the aftershocks of that moment in the mind of God, as photons of light arrive from the most distant galaxies.[2] Thus,

[1] R. B. English, "Democritus' Theory of Sense Perception," *Transactions and Proceedings of the American Philological Association* 46 (1915): 217–27.

[2] See, for example, this image from the Hubble Space Telescope: *http://hubblesite.org/newscenter/archive/releases/2004/07/image/a/*.

the phenomenon of touch may have the broadest implications of all the senses, especially in the context of the incarnation, in which God became matter so that he could *touch* and thereby heal his creation.

In the theophany that Moses experienced at the burning bush (plate 1), God initiates his relationship with Moses in a dramatic way. Drawn initially by the sense of sight, Moses approaches the burning yet unconsumed bush. God calls Moses from the bush, and Moses responds verbally, saying, "Here am I," and thus assenting to the beginning of the relationship. However, it is God's next statement that defines the relationship: "Do not come near; put off your shoes from your feet, for the place on which you are standing is holy ground." The Fathers of the Church have interpreted God's command for Moses to remove his shoes in different ways. In writing of repentance, St Ambrose of Milan (+397) uses this *putting off of shoes* as a metaphor for the repentant to free themselves from attachments in this life: "For if it is said to Moses when he was desiring to draw nearer: 'Put off thy shoes from off thy feet,' how much more must we free the feet of our soul from the bonds of the body, and clear our steps from all connection with this world."[3] Regarding the second half of this passage, Ambrose makes a powerful analogy between the holy ground upon which Moses stood and a steadfast faith and commitment to the Church.[4] Late in his life, St Gregory Nazianzus, one of the fourth-century Cappadocian fathers, referred to this encounter between Moses and God in his last Easter homily, in which he reviewed the first Jewish Passover's allegorical significance for Christians. "And as to the shoes, let him who is about to touch the Holy Land which the feet of God have trodden, put them off, as Moses did upon the Mount, that he may bring there nothing dead; nothing to come between Man and God."[5] At that time, shoes (sandals) typically were made from the skin (leather) of dead animals, and no dead thing should serve as a barrier to this direct encounter with the living God.

[3] St Ambrose, *Concerning Repentance* 2.11.107, in vol. 10 of Nicene and Post-Nicene Fathers [henceforth NPNF], Second Series, ed. Philip Schaff and Henry Wace (Peabody, MA: Hendrickson Publishers, 1994), 358–59.

[4] Ibid., Letter 63.41–42 (NPNF[2] 10:462).

[5] St Gregory Nazianzus, *The Second Oration on Easter* 19 (NPNF[2] 7:430).

What are the elements that make up this barrier of mortality between God and man? Essentially, anything that distracts one from the encounter with God—that draws one away from life toward death, that acts as a barrier between one and the Source of life—represents the shoes that must be removed. Within the spiritual Tradition of the Church, the passions are these barriers separating the human person from God. Evagrius of Pontus (+399) makes this very clear: "When Moses tried to draw near to the burning bush he was forbidden to approach until he had loosed his sandals from his feet. If, then, you wish to behold and commune with Him who is beyond sense-perception and beyond concept, you must free yourself from every impassioned thought."[6] Herein lies a great paradox so fundamental to incarnational theology. In this scriptural passage, the Church sees the preincarnate Word of God speaking to Moses from the burning bush. The bush has been transfigured by the fire of the divine presence, revealing that matter can indeed be touched and illuminated by the holy. This is a foretaste of the transfiguration of Christ on Mt Tabor, where Moses was also present. It is a beginning of the journey culminating in the Word become flesh (Jn 1.14). This encounter between Moses and God begins to repair the break in the relationship between the first humans and God. After their sin, Adam and Eve hid from God in their nakedness when he called out to them (Gen 3.9), whereas Moses, when called by God, removed his sandals at God's command so that his naked feet might directly contact the ground made holy by God's presence. God seeks out fallen man in the person of Moses and restores the intimacy of paradise in his command to remove the sandals so that there will be no barrier, physical or spiritual, between his creature and himself.

In this image of the bush, burning but not consumed, the Church has also seen a type of the Virgin Mary's bearing the incarnate Word of God within her womb. The great sixth-century Byzantine poet and hymnographer St Romanus stated this most beautifully in his *kontakion* (hymn) *On the Mother of God*:

[6]Evagrius the Solitary, *On Prayer: One Hundred and Fifty-Three Texts* 4, in *Philokalia* 1:57–58.

> As once there was a fire in the bush shining brightly and not
> burning the thorn,
> so now the Lord is in the Virgin.
> For God did not wish to delude Moses or to terrify him,
> but, making known to him what was to come in the future,
> he showed the bush bearing fire, that
> he might learn that, to Christ
> *a Virgin gives birth, and after childbirth remains*
> *still a virgin.*[7]

By virtue of the Virgin's perfect obedience and full communion with the Word of God made flesh within her womb, she made it possible for all her children in the Church also to receive and bear God within themselves. This carrying of God who is Spirit within each Christian occurs through the paradox of intimate contact with the material. "Take, eat; this is my Body" (Mt 26.26) can only have real meaning when God becomes touchable in the incarnation. Then, and only then, is it possible for St Symeon the New Theologian to say in his prayer before communion, "I partake of fire, being grass, and behold a strange wonder, I am unexpectedly refreshed as was the burning bush, burning but not consumed."[8]

It is this sanctification of the material through the incarnation of Christ that has made the veneration of icons possible, not as objects of worship in and of themselves, but as representations that make present the person or event portrayed. Ultimately, all icons must point to Christ. St John of Damascus, the great eighth-century defender of icons, said, "I do not venerate matter, I venerate the fashioner of matter, who became matter for my sake, and in matter made his abode, and through matter worked my salvation. . . . I reverence therefore matter and I hold in respect and venerate that through which my salvation has

---

[7]St Romanus the Melodist, *On the Mother of God*, in *On the Life of Christ: Kontakia* trans. Ephrem Lash (San Francisco: HarperCollins Publishers, 1995), 19.

[8]St Symeon the New Theologian, "Seventh Prayer before the Service of Holy Communion," in *Daily Prayers for Orthodox Christians: The Synekdemos*, ed. N. Michael Vaporis (Brookline, MA: Holy Cross Orthodox Press, 1986), 92.

come about, I reverence it not as God, but as filled with divine energy and grace."[9] Thus, with discernment one can truly see the icon (image) of God in each human person and can encounter the energies of God in those elements that have been touched by the divine. The ultimate destiny for every Christian is to become by grace what God is by nature, to participate in the divine life to the fullest extent possible for creatures. This is true healing, real health. At the heart of this process of what is known as *theosis* in the Eastern Church is the relationship between God, who is pure spirit, and his material creature. The incarnation has materialized the spiritual so that the material can be spiritualized. This could not happen without touch.

By his very nature, God desires an intimacy with his creation that could only be achieved by becoming material, by uniting himself to his creation, even his fallen creation. In this act he made it possible for the ordinary to become extraordinary. This transformation occurs through the senses. In the Church's liturgical worship, words become transfigured into healing sounds from the Spirit of God, touching the faithful like the fiery tongues of Pentecost. The smell of incense becomes the wordless prayer of the body of Christ ascending back in thanksgiving and glory to God. The taste of the bread and wine becomes the intimate kiss of peace between wounded creature and loving Healer. All of these physical and sensual experiences establish a continuity of contact, a healing relationship between Creator and creature.

This book will explore the crucial role of the sense of touch in the process of *theosis* through reflections on a series of icons in which touch is a central element. Each chapter will be informed by a reflection on individual icons that highlight a specific aspect of touch and its relationship to the healing ministry of Christ.

[9]St John of Damascus, *Three Treatises on the Divine Images* 2.14 (PPS 24:70–71).

Plate 2

CHAPTER I

The Maternal Embrace

The captain of the angelic hosts was sent by God Almighty to the pure Virgin to announce the good tidings of a strange and secret wonder: that God as man would be born a child of her without seed, fashioning again the whole human race! Proclaim, people, the good tidings of the re-creation of the world!

—Anonymous[1]

THIS QUOTE FROM THE LITURGY of the Feast of the Annunciation summarizes succinctly and powerfully the strange and marvelous hope embedded within the truth of the incarnation. The primal disobedience of the first Eve is undone by the perfect obedience of the Virgin Mary in her assent to the message of the angelic messenger. For the early Fathers of the Church, Eve represented a negative type of the Virgin Mary; Mary becomes the new Eve, the mother of a new creation. Commenting on chapter 3 of Genesis, Irenaeus, a second-century bishop of Lyon, emphasizes this parallel but opposite relationship:

> As Eve was seduced by the word of a [fallen] angel to flee from God, having rebelled against his word, so Mary by the word of an angel received the glad tidings that she would bear God by obeying his word. The former was seduced to disobey God [and so fell], but the latter was persuaded to obey God, so that the Virgin Mary might become the advocate of the virgin Eve. As the human race was subjected to death through the act of a virgin, so was it saved by a virgin, and thus the disobedience of one virgin was precisely balanced by the obedience of another.[2]

[1]Anonymous, Exaposteilarion of the Annunciation, in ACCS:NT 3:16.
[2]Irenaeus, *Against Heresies* 5.19.1, in ACCS:OT 1:78–79.

The *second Eve* cooperates fully with the healing, re-creative act of God and becomes the source of the humanity for the Word made flesh (Jn 1). She, in effect, becomes the mother of a new humanity in the person of Jesus Christ. Broken, sinful humanity, a "failed creation," finds its source of healing through the obedience and humility of this one woman.

The fourth-century theologian and bishop Gregory of Nyssa likens the predicament of the fallen creation to that of someone who has been fooled into taking poison:

> Those who have been tricked into taking poison offset its harmful effect by another drug. The remedy, moreover, just like the poison, has to enter the system, so that its remedial effect may thereby spread through the whole body. Similarly, having tasted the poison, that is the fruit, that dissolved our nature, we were necessarily in need of something to reunite it. Such a remedy had to enter into us, so that it might by its counteraction undo the harm the body had already encountered from the poison. And what is this remedy? Nothing else than the body that proved itself superior to death and became the source of life.[3]

For God in his mercy to heal his "sick" creation, the only solution was to unite himself fully with it and thereby transform it from within. This meant embracing, in his infinite humility, all aspects of our humanity except for sin. Thus, he comes born of a virgin in the fullness of time. The original Creator, the Word of God, enters his own sick and wounded creation to become a new Adam, to restore and heal the cosmos. St Athanasius, the great fourth-century defender of Christian orthodoxy, beautifully describes this marvelous paradox of the uncontainable God contained within a human body: "And the most wonderful thing was that he both sojourned as a human being, and as the Word begot life in everything, and as Son was with the Father."[4] He became

---

[3]Gregory of Nyssa, *Address on Religious Instruction* 37, in ACCS:OT 1:78.

[4]St Athanasius, *On the Incarnation* 17, in *On the Incarnation: Greek Original and English Translation*, trans. John Behr, PPS 44a (Crestwood, NY: St Vladimir's Seminary Press, 2011), 87.

a man to accomplish two things: to re-create the human person by destroying the power of death and to reveal "himself ... [as] the Word of the Father" to his creation.[5]

God's intimate embrace of his suffering creation—indeed, his assumption of all our suffering and mortality as the crucified Lord of Glory—is foundational to any understanding of healing in the traditional Christian sense. A central element in this deep mystery of God's love for his creation is the special relationship between the incarnate Word of God and his mother, the Virgin Mary. "I will put enmity between you and the woman, and between your seed and her seed; he shall bruise your head, and you shall bruise his heel" (Gen 3.15). The early fathers saw in this passage from Genesis a reference to Christ's ultimate victory over the devil. The mutual love and deep compassion that exist between Mary and her Son make possible this victory for the renewed creation:

> Christ completely renewed all things, both taking up the battle against our enemy and crushing him who at the beginning had led us captive in Adam, trampling on his head, as you find in Genesis that God said to the serpent, "I will put enmity between you and the woman. . . ." From then on it was proclaimed that he who was to be born of a virgin, after the likeness of Adam, would be on the watch for the serpent's head. . . . The enemy would not have been justly conquered unless it had been a man made of woman who conquered him. For it was by a woman that he had power over man from the beginning, setting himself up in opposition to man. Because of this the Lord also declares himself to be the Son of Man, so renewing in himself that primal man from whom the formation of man by woman began ... and as death won the palm of victory over us by a man, so we might by a man receive the palm of victory over death.[6]

[5] *On the Incarnation* 16, ibid., 85.
[6] Irenaeus, *Against Heresies* 5.21.1, in ACCS:OT 1:90–91.

As Love, God chooses to abase himself in fully experiencing the weakness and vulnerability of an infant so that in this supreme act of humility, he can break down the barrier between the creature and Creator. His embrace as a helpless, dependent child of his mother very specifically clarifies the type of intimate reconciliation and healing he desires with his creatures. He takes the initiative; he makes himself vulnerable, in every sense of the word. He who holds the universe in his hand voluntarily makes himself dependent for life and sustenance on his own creature and then reaches out to her in the innocent embrace of a child, creating the possibility that every similar act could be transformed into a moment of grace-filled healing.

Icons of the Virgin Mary and her Son within the Orthodox Tradition highlight different aspects of this intimate healing relationship between mother and Son, between creature and Creator. Two major forms of the iconographic depiction of the Virgin and Child in the Eastern tradition are that of the *Hodigitria* and *Eleousa*.[7] The two styles illustrate in visual form the profound depth and subtle features of the relationship between the Mother of God and her Child. In icons of the *Hodigitria* type, Mary is often depicted in a reflective stance, looking out at the viewer and pointing the way (or being the "guide," *Hodigitria* in Greek) to Christ her Son. Sorrow may be reflected in her eyes as she contemplates her Son's mission and future suffering, while the facial expression of the Child Christ already embodies the mature Savior who offers his blessing to the world. While many of these elements are also present in the *Eleousa* (from the Greek for "compassionate" or "merciful one") type icon, it incorporates an additional element that transcends the theological statement about the incarnation of the Word of God made by icons of the *Hodigitria* type: the *Eleousa*-type icon reveals the human emotions shared in the relationship between the Mother of God and her Son. The powerful expression of the emotional

[7]For an excellent discussion of the different types of icons depicting the Virgin Mary as the Mother of God, see Leonid Ouspensky and Vladimir Lossky, *The Meaning of Icons*, trans. G. E. H. Palmer and E. Kadloubovsky, 2nd ed. (Crestwood, NY: St Vladimir's Seminary Press, 1999), 76–103.

response between mother and Son in icons of the *Eleousa* type confirms the full condescension of the divine to the human that occurred with the incarnation.

The icon known as the Vladimir Mother of God, a type of *Eleousa* icon (see figure 1 and plate 2, which is modeled on this icon), has a long history. Indeed, it (or the style it typifies) may be very old. There is a tradition that it was painted by St Luke the Evangelist, who is credited as the first iconographer. It was sent to Russia in the twelfth century from Byzantium and eventually became associated with the city of Vladimir, north of Kiev, after its transport there by a Russian prince. This icon has been credited with the rescue of Russia from the Tatars on several occasions. This icon emphasizes the mutual affection and tenderness expressed between Son and mother in their close contact. This embrace of Son and mother is a visible, *tangible* reflection of the simultaneous, invisible union existing between the Son and his Father, which St Athanasius described. The gentle, tender, and very physical love of a child for its mother has received the ultimate benediction. When one contemplates this image, the mystery hidden within the embrace of every child and its mother is revealed. God has a maternal love for his creation, and this maternal tenderness is also felt within the relationship of the persons of the Holy Trinity. God the Father, in effect, is offering the Virgin Mary the opportunity to become the image or model of his tender, maternal love for the helpless and vulnerable. His Son's image is present in each child, in each vulnerable person. The model we are to emulate specifically includes a physical element. We must not only—in some very real sense—be willing to touch the other, but we must also not be inhibited in our care and compassion; the touch must not be a tentative form of contact.

Physical contact is a fundamental aspect of living. At a very basic level, even contact between many types of cells, either with each other or with their local environment (extracellular matrix), is essential to their survival.[8] Indeed, the loss of normal cell-to-cell contact or cell

[8]Cf. S. M. Frisch and E. Ruoslahti, "Integrins and Anoikis," *Current Opinion in Cell Biology* 9 (1997): 701–6; and R. C. Bates, A. Buret, E. F. van Helden, M. A.

contact with the extracellular matrix (the normal site of attachment of cells in tissues) creates a state called *anoikis* (Greek), cellular "homelessness," that induces programmed cell death or *apoptosis* (Greek). In their transformation to the malignant state, cancer cells typically overcome or inactivate the signals that are associated with *anoikis*, allowing for the possibility of metastatic spread of the cancer to other tissues. Thus, under normal circumstances, contact or touch at the most basic level provides a stabilizing, healthy influence within an organism.

Scientific studies of touch presented in the form of gentle pressure have demonstrated remarkable effects on growth and development in animal models as well as in premature and even healthy human infants.[9] The application of pressure—real contact between "healer" and "patient"—appears to be critical to the therapeutic effect. Thus, the vigorous licking of a rat pup by its mother or the stroking, kissing, and hugging of a small infant by a loved one or nurse may act through neurohumoral pathways to stimulate release of growth hormone and reduce the production of stress hormones, among other effects. There is a reciprocal character to the benefits derived from massage. Elderly volunteers trained to massage healthy infants have experienced improvement in affect and a reduction in anxiety as a byproduct of their tangible interactions with the infants.[10] By nature, we are created for physical contact with others.

In the *Eleousa* icon, the embrace between the *Theotokos* (Greek, the one who gives birth to God) and her Son signifies a whole range of shared human emotions, including fear, pain, sorrow, trust, hope, comfort, and unconditional love. In this very human action of the Theotokos and her Son, all the conflicting emotions are resolved. The human-divine contact portrayed in this icon is a powerful image of

Horton, and G. F. Burns, "Apoptosis Induced by Inhibition of Intercellular Contact," *Journal of Cell Biology* 125.2 (1994): 403–15; 9:701–70.

[9]For excellent overviews, please see T. Field, "Enhancing Growth," *Touch Therapy* (London: Churchill Livingstone, 2000); and A. Montagu, *Touching: The Human Significance of the Skin*, 3rd ed. (New York: HarperCollins, 1986).

[10]Ibid.

reconciliation between God and his creation. The loving embrace that is shared between Christ and his mother—despite the shadow of all the suffering to come—is an image of the ineffable love flowing between the Persons of the Holy Trinity, a love that mystically embraces the entire cosmos in its suffering and need for healing.

The universal character of the mercy and compassion that are embodied in the *Eleousa*-type icon of the Mother of God is best described in a passage from St Isaac of Syria's homilies (seventh century), in which he describes the nature of a merciful heart:

> It is the heart's burning for the sake of the entire creation, for men, for birds, for animals, for demons, and for every created thing; and by the recollection and sight of them the eyes of a merciful man pour forth abundant tears. From the strong and vehement mercy, which grips his heart and from his great compassion, his heart is humbled and he cannot bear to hear or to see any injury or slight sorrow in creation. For this reason he offers up tearful prayer continually even for irrational beasts, for the enemies of the truth, and for those who harm him, that they may be protected and receive mercy. And in like manner he even prays for the family of reptiles because of the great compassion that burns without measure in his heart in the likeness of God.[11]

This is the all-embracing compassion and mercy that are expressed in the *Eleousa*-type icon of the Mother of God.

Something else becomes quite evident when one more closely examines the *Eleousa* icon (plate 2). While tenderly embracing her Son, the Virgin at the same time engages the viewer with a look of deep sorrow that is fully intermingled with the love she bears for her Son. But, if one continues to meet her gaze, steadily without distraction, one may also see that the sorrowful love embodied in her maternal embrace is being offered in a very direct and personal manner to the viewer. The new Eve offers her loving embrace and protection to all her children, declaring,

[11]St Isaac of Syria, Homily 71, in *Ascetical Homilies of Saint Isaac the Syrian* (Boston, MA: Holy Transfiguration Monastery, 1984), 344–45.

"My soul magnifies the Lord, and my spirit rejoices in God my Savior, for he has regarded the low estate of His handmaiden. For behold, henceforth all generations will call me blessed; for he who is mighty has done great things for me, and holy is his name. And his mercy is on those who fear him from generation to generation" (Lk 1.46–50).

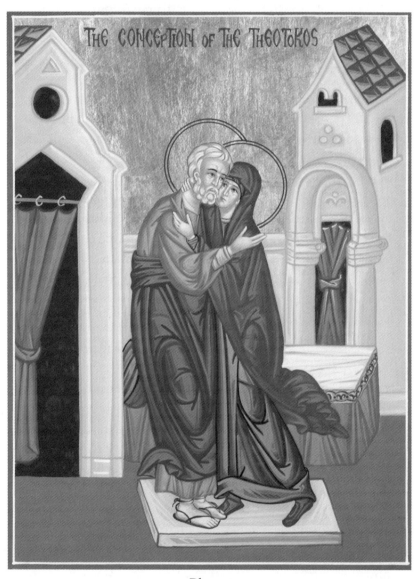

Plate 3

CHAPTER 2

Love's Embrace

The body can be defiled by the merest touch, for of all the senses this is the most dangerous.
— St John Climacus, *The Ladder of Divine Ascent*[1]

O that you would kiss me with the kisses of your mouth!
— Song of Solomon 1.2 (RSV)

T HESE TWO QUOTATIONS reflect the ambivalence regarding human sexuality that has existed within the Christian tradition from the beginning. The first, from the sixth-century spiritual classic, sums up the intense anxiety of many of the Church fathers concerning the negative impact of human sensuality on the spiritual life, while the second, from the Song of Songs, has been endorsed enthusiastically by those same fathers, but primarily as spiritual metaphor. Thus, the Christian tradition has emphasized that the physicality described so vividly in the Song of Songs is to be primarily understood within the context of the hidden, ineffable mysteries of the love that exists between God and his Church and between God and each individual soul. And yet, like so many other mysteries of the Church, is it possible that the physical type of the spiritual antitype might in its own right be good and even blessed by God?

In the iconographic tradition of the Church, the icon of the conception of the Virgin Mary,[2] the conception of the Theotokos, is very

[1] St John Climacus, The Ladder of Divine Ascent, trans. Colm Luibheid and Norman Russell (Mahwah, NJ: Paulist Press, 1982), 178.
[2] The ancient tradition describing the conception of the Virgin Mary is recorded in a very early source, probably from the second century, the *Protoevangelium (or Infancy Gospel) of St James*. For the text, see M. R. James, *The Apocryphal New Testament* (London: Oxford University Press, 1966), 38–49.

discreet in its depiction of human sexuality (see plate 3). An embrace and an implied kiss exchanged by the elderly husband and wife, Joachim and Anna, are sufficient to depict with all modesty their coming together to conceive the Theotokos. A central feature of the icon is movement—not a random movement, but one that is clearly expressing direction and intentionality. The barren couple, in response to the promise of God, approach and embrace each other in faith. The desire and passion of youth may have been winnowed by the years, but the intensity of their commitment to each other is stronger than ever. They now come together physically in the manner of husband and wife and perform, through conviction and trust, an act that previously may have been motivated primarily by desire. When even the possibility of conception was logically beyond reach, they now conceive through obedience to the divine directive. Thus, the physical pleasure of sexual union is blessed by its deference to selfless love.

Within the modest embrace exchanged between Joachim and Anna, as depicted in the icon, are hidden great truths about love. The iconographic tradition of the Church has placed a veil over this profound mystery, to guard and preserve it—a notion quite foreign to modern sensibilities, in which the whole phenomenon is often reduced to mere biological drives. For more than the act of physical relations between husband and wife is portrayed here. In one sense, the kiss represents the traditional "kiss of peace" that persons of good will might exchange, but in this instance the peace that is exchanged is the grace of God, working in the mutual love and obedience of husband and wife that will bear such extraordinary fruit in the greatest of human conceptions. Just as God suspended the laws of creation in his divine-human incarnation, in the conception of his Mother—this act of obedient love—he also has blessed the mystery inherent within the physiological process of human conception by creating the new Eve.

The first three chapters of the book of Genesis have been a rich and deep vein that the Fathers of the Church mined extensively for its spiritual wisdom, especially regarding the origin of sin and the mystery of the relationship between the masculine and feminine members of the human race. While many of the fathers have emphasized that the major purpose of sexual intercourse is procreation, there have always been allusions to a deeper meaning and purpose, starting with St Paul's assertion that the "two becoming one flesh" (Gen 2.24) is "a great mystery . . . of Christ and the Church" (Eph 5.32). So, although the two practical reasons for marriage often given by the fathers have been the begetting of children and chastity (to prevent fornication),[3] the same fathers have recognized other reasons as well. In speaking against marriage as a means of acquiring wealth, St John Chrysostom (+407) pointedly asserts, "Marriage is not a business venture but a *fellowship for life*."[4] In commenting on Genesis 2.18, Tertullian (+220) does not exclude pleasure from God's plan to provide a helper for the man:

> Goodness annexed pleasures to man; so that, while master of the whole world, he might tarry among higher delights, being translated into paradise, out of the world into the Church. The self-same Goodness provided also a help meet for him, that there might be nothing in his lot that was not good. For said He, that the man to be alone is not good. He knew full well what a blessing to him would be the sex of Mary, and also of the Church.[5]

On one level the fathers confirm that the woman is created as a helper in generation of more human beings, but as can be seen in the quote from Tertullian, there was also recognition that the role of *helper* implies something more profound beyond the generation of children, perhaps someone with whom to share the God-given pleasures, which lead to higher delights.

The deeper meaning of "helper" is hidden within the mystery of the creation of man described in Genesis. Although all the animals came before Adam to be named by him, none was found to be an appropriate

---

[3]For example, St John Chrysostom, "Sermon on Marriage," in *On Marriage and Family Life*, PPS 7 (Crestwood, NY: St Vladimir's Seminary Press, 1991), 85.

[4]St John Chrysostom, "How to Choose a Wife," in *On Marriage and Family Life*, 96 (emphasis added).

[5]Tertullian, *Against Marcion* 3, in ANF 3:300.

helper for him (Gen 2.20). The creation of the human being was only completed when the woman was fashioned out of the man's rib so that he then could declare her to be, indeed, "bone of my bone, and flesh of my flesh" (Gen 2.23). Whereas all of the other creatures and the man were created from the dust of the ground, the woman acquired her existence from man, for she was fully present in Adam before she was fashioned from his rib. Later, in the divine symmetry, the new Adam, Jesus Christ, would acquire his flesh and human existence from the Virgin Mary, the new Eve. St Augustine (+430) expands upon this theme by further emphasizing the woman's fully shared humanity with the man:

> For at the beginning of the human race the woman was made of a rib taken from the side of the man while he slept; for it seemed fit that even then Christ and His Church should be foreshadowed in this event. For that sleep of the man was the death of Christ, whose side, as He hung lifeless upon the cross, was pierced with a spear, and there flowed from it blood and water, and these we know to be the sacraments by which the Church is "built up." For Scripture used this very word, not saying He "formed" or "framed," but "built her up into a woman;" whence also the apostle speaks of the *edification* of the body of Christ [Eph 4.12], which is the Church. The woman, therefore, is a creature of God, even as the man; *but by her creation from man unity is commended* [emphasis added]; and the manner of her creation prefigured . . . Christ and the Church.[6]

What precisely is this unity that is commended? On one most fundamental level, it is the unity of the feminine and masculine aspects of the human person, which were both fully present in Adam before Eve was formed from his rib. St Ephrem the Syrian (+373) clarifies the unique nature of this new creation this way: "God then took her and brought her to Adam who was both one and two: he was one because he was Adam, and he was two because he was created male and female."[7]

[6] St Augustine, *The City of God* 22.17 (NPNF[1] 2:496).
[7] St Ephrem the Syrian, *The Commentary on Genesis* 2.12, in *Hymns on Paradise*, trans. Sebastian Brock, PPS 10 (Crestwood, NY: St Vladimir's Seminary Press, 1990), 205.

Developing this theme further, St Ephrem adds, "Seeing that all species of animals had received from him a name on that very day, Adam
did not call the rib that had been fashioned by her personal name 'Eve,'
but called her instead 'woman,' the generic name applying to her entire
kind. He said, 'a man shall leave his father and his mother and attach
himself to his wife' so that they might be united and the two become
one, without division, as they were originally."[8]

In some sense, male and female sexuality embodies the tension
between the active and passive aspects within each human person.
Thus, the roles that St Paul describes (Eph 5.22ff.)—of male as *head*
and female as *body* subject in deference to the head—are unitive functions of the whole person. St John Chrysostom explains that within the
married state the different roles are not indicative of greater or lesser
dignity on the part of the man or woman, saying, "Paul places the head
in authority and the body in obedience for the sake of peace. Where
there is equal authority, there is never peace. A household cannot be a
democracy, ruled by everyone, but the authority must necessarily rest
in one person."[9] When marriage is realized to be a type of the Church
as the body of Christ in which each member is "married" to Christ,
it becomes clear that both male and female members of the body are
equally subject to Christ, the head. The lay theologian Philip Sherrard
described the androgynous human creature prior to division into male
and female as bearing the fullness of the image of the Creator.[10] Thus,
the union of man and woman in marriage restores the primordial unity
of the masculine and feminine aspects of the human person as created
in the image of God.

---

[8]Ibid., 206. It is important to note that in the Septuagint, in the passage quoted by
St Ephrem from Genesis 2.24, it is the human being (*anthrōpos*, Greek), who departs
from father and mother to achieve union as one flesh with the woman. Marriage,
then, is a reuniting of both the feminine and masculine aspects of the human person
to create a new and whole creature.

[9]St John Chrysostom, Homily 20 on Ephesians 5.22–23, in *On Marriage and
Family Life*, 53.

[10]Philip Sherrard, *Christianity and Eros: Essays on the Theme of Sexual Love*
(Limni, Evia, Greece: Denise Harvey Publisher, 1995), 55ff.

The union of man and woman may result in the creation of new life. St John Chrysostom extends the unity of man and woman to the child born of their union as an image of communion with Christ. "The child is born from the union of their seed, so the three are one flesh. Our relationship to Christ is the same; we become one flesh with Him through communion, more truly one with Him than our children are one with us, because this has been His plan from the beginning."[11] In fact, according to St John, a Christian home can constitute in microcosm the fullness of the Church.[12] It can also become an icon of the Holy Trinity to the extent that the relationships within the marriage and family are nurtured and sustained by a fully shared, reciprocal love that completely transcends self and finds fulfillment and joy in the other. Thus, he goes on to say with regard to the selfishness that often accompanies the union of husband and wife, "You no longer have a body of your own (since you gave it away in marriage), yet you have money of your own? After marriage, you are no longer two, but one flesh, and are your possessions still divided? Love of money! You have both become one person, one organism, and can you still say, 'my own'? This cursed and abominable phrase comes from the devil."[13] Marriage can then be seen in this light as a powerful remedy for the solitary self-absorption of the ego.

Returning to the question posed at the beginning of this chapter, is it possible to reconcile the deep concerns within the Tradition regarding erotic pleasure in marriage with its spiritual antitype, the love of Christ for the Church? Interestingly, St John Chrysostom makes some remarkable assertions related to the love expressed between husband and wife, including the physical aspects of that relationship. He not only advises the husband on how to speak with real terms of endearment to his wife, but also emphasizes how the husband's treatment

[11]St John Chrysostom, Homily 20 on Ephesians 5.22–23, in *On Marriage and Family Life*, 51.
[12]Ibid., 57.
[13]Ibid., 62.

of his wife lays the foundation for the joys of eternity together in the kingdom of heaven:

> Tell her that you love her more than your own life, because this present life is nothing, and that your only hope is that the two of you pass through this life in such a way that *in the world to come you will be united in perfect love.* Say to her, "Our time here is brief and fleeting, but if we are pleasing to God, we can exchange this life for the Kingdom to come. Then we will be perfectly one both with Christ and with each other, and *our pleasure will know no bounds.*"[14]

It is hard to imagine that there is no connection between the perfect unity in love between husband and wife and, in turn, their unity with Christ and St John's statement that "our pleasure will know no bounds." In the Septuagint version of the formation of Eve from the rib of Adam (Gen 2.21), God causes him to enter literally into a state of ecstasy (*ekstasin*, Greek), and then he sleeps during the divine procedure. Could not the intense physical joy and pleasure of sexual union—in which there is complete loss of self in the mutual giving between husband and wife within the sacramental grace of marriage—represent a recapitulation of the ecstasy of Adam at the creation of Eve from his deepest self? What the Creator had divided is now fully reunited as one complete being in divinely blessed erotic love.

St Ephrem the Syrian insisted on the absolute necessity of the senses, including that of touch, for humans to fully develop spiritually as they encounter reality—and especially ultimate reality in the life of Paradise, albeit through a transformed physicality in the resurrection body. "If the soul, while in the body, resembles an embryo and is unable to know either itself or its companion, how much more feeble will it then be once it has left the body, no longer possessing on its own the senses which are able to serve as tools for it to use. For it is through the senses of its companion that it shines forth and becomes evident."[15] And then, continuing with a description of the resurrection body in

---

[14]Ibid., 61 (emphasis added).
[15]St Ephrem the Syrian, Hymn 8.6, *Hymns on Paradise*, 133.

paradise, he says, "That blessed abode is in no way deficient, for that place is complete and perfected in every way, and the soul cannot enter there alone, for in such a state it is in everything deficient—in sensation and consciousness; but on the day of Resurrection the body, with all its senses, will enter in as well, once it has been made perfect."[16]

Many of the fathers write at length concerning the birth of the passions with the fall of the first humans. Whereas before the fall Adam and Eve were unaware of their nakedness and were "covered" by glory, after they disobeyed and ate from the Tree of the Knowledge of Good and Evil, they were now acutely aware of their naked state. The passions arose out of distortion of normal impulses and sensory functions through disobedience:

> Eve is the first to teach us that sight, taste and the other senses, when used without moderation, distract the heart from its remembrance of God. So long as she did not look with longing at the forbidden tree, she was able to keep God's commandment carefully in mind; she was still covered by the wings of divine love and thus was ignorant of her own nakedness. But after she had looked at the tree with longing, touched it with ardent desire and then tasted its fruit with active sensuality, she at once felt drawn to physical intercourse and, being naked, she gave way to her passion.[17]

St Augustine makes a crucial distinction between the unrestrained desire occasioned by the fall and what might have been realized if the first couple had not fallen but rather had grown together physically and spiritually in obedience to God's command. "Why, therefore, may we not assume that the first couple before they sinned could have given a command to their genital organs for the purpose of procreation as they did to the other members that the soul is accustomed to move to perform various tasks without any trouble and without any craving for

---

[16]Ibid., Hymn 8.7, *Hymns on Paradise*, 133–34.
[17]St Diadochus of Photiki (fifth century), *On Spiritual Knowledge and Discernment: One Hundred Texts* 56, in *Philokalia* 1:261.

pleasure?"[18] Here the problem appears to be *craving for pleasure* rather than pleasure per se. Following this reasoning a bit further, Adam and Eve could have chosen the fruit of any other tree in the garden and, commanding their limbs to acquire it and place it in proximity to their mouths, could have tasted, eaten, and consumed it with pleasure. It is the powerful desire—the craving that is no longer subject to reason and an obedient love—that can lead to the selfish transformation of persons into objects to be used to achieve one's own pleasure. The pleasure itself is a gift from God, which, through the distorted lens of the passion of lust, is now tainted.

In contemplating the icon of the conception of the Theotokos, we see that the vision of St Augustine of a paradisiacal procreation has been fulfilled in the coming together of this faithful, elderly couple who, in obedience to God, conceive the new Eve. Their embrace has reconciled chastity with continent pleasure. If we further reflect upon the human relationship that is portrayed in the icon, is there not an additional level of meaning to be drawn from it as a type of the love of Christ for the members of his body, the Church? Is it possible that the embrace of Sts Joachim and Anna also signifies the deepest form of empathy, an ever-more-intimate and joyful (and even pleasurable) encounter with God in the never-ending process of growth and participation by grace in the divine life known as deification (*theosis*, Greek)? In her study of St Ephrem, Susan Ashbrook Harvey has emphasized St Ephrem's insistence on the critical importance of sensory experience in truly knowing the other.

> We know first by encounter, by bodily experience, before we can process understanding . . . rational thought positions a person apart from the object of consideration. What Ephrem describes is an encounter between subject and object in which the person will be saturated at every level of awareness and being by the object sought, to the point where the subjective encounter is swallowed up by the

[18]St Augustine, *On the Literal Interpretation of Genesis* 9.10.18, in ACCS:OT 1:93–94.

immensity of presence in the midst of what is divine . . . the human self is not lost in this event, nor obliterated by the power of God's Being. Rather, here is a relationship between creature and Creator of completion, of full realization of self within Self. The resurrected life is that condition in which nothing separates us from God.[19]

As the twentieth-century Christian apologist C. S. Lewis pointed out so well, *eros*, or romantic love, can come close to fulfilling the command to love one's neighbor as oneself for at least one other person. Lewis says, "It is an image, a foretaste, of what we must become to all if Love Himself rules in us without a rival."[20] It is precisely the intensity of the commitment, the powerful empathy that is formed between those "in love," that must be transferable to all of one's relationships, but most especially with God. One must not "fall out of love" in one's relationship with the divine and with the image of the divine that is borne in the suffering countenance of one's neighbor.

In that discreet kiss of the aging lovers, who conceived through God's grace the Mother of the God-Man, is a sign of the mysterious love that each person can experience in the encounter with God and one's neighbor. Thus, the celibate monastic can appropriate the imagery and language of romantic love. In the Song of Songs, the bride speaks of being wounded with love in her deep yearning for the bridegroom (Song 2.5, LXX). It is this intensity of love described in the romantic language of the senses that each Christian soul is called to experience empathically. The fourth-century Western Church father St Ambrose speaks about the nature of the wound of love inflicted by God: "The Word of God inflicts a wound, but it does not produce a sore. There is a wound of righteous love, there are wounds of charity, as she has said [in reference to Song 2.5], 'I am wounded with love.' The one who is perfect is wounded with love. Therefore the wounds of the Word are good, and good are the wounds of the lover."[21] It is in this spirit that

---

[19]S. A. Harvey, "Embodiment in Time and Eternity: A Syriac Perspective," *St Vladimir's Theological Quarterly* 43 (1999): 125–26, at 105–30.

[20]C. S. Lewis, *The Four Loves* (London: Collins Fontana Books, 1974), 105.

[21]St Ambrose of Milan, *On Virginity* 14.91, in ACCS:OT 9:313.

every Christian soul can vicariously assume the words of the bride. The sense of touch is the starting point for what can become the ecstatic encounter with God in the mystery of his love.

Plate 4

CHAPTER 3

Healing through Material Means

He gave us divinity, we gave Him humanity.

—St Ephrem the Syrian[1]

As he passed by, he saw a man blind from his birth. And his disciples asked him, "Rabbi, who sinned, this man or his parents, that he was born blind?" Jesus answered, "It was not that this man sinned, or his parents, but that the works of God might be made manifest in him. We[2] must work the works of him who sent me." . . . He spat on the ground and made clay of the spittle and anointed the man's eyes with the clay."

—John 9.1–4, 6 (*See plate 4*)

W HY DID CHRIST go to all the trouble of spitting on the ground, making mud, and then applying it to the eyes of the blind man? There were many other instances recorded in the Gospels in which he merely spoke a word, healing at a distance without touching his patient. What was so different about this situation? Of the limited number of signs (*sēmeia*, Greek) recorded in St John's Gospel "so that you might believe that Jesus is the Christ, the Son of God" (Jn 20.31), why did the evangelist choose this particular sign?

The Church fathers emphasize the uniqueness of this healing miracle in their commentaries. There were certainly other instances in which Christ miraculously cured blindness,[3] but in the other cases the blindness had been acquired during life. In John 9 the man had been born with defective, unformed, or partially formed eyes. His ophthalmic malformation was a reflection of a creation that was incomplete.

---

[1]St Ephrem the Syrian, *Hymns on Faith* 5.17, quoted in *Hymns on Paradise*, 74.
[2]Variant reading from early texts (e.g., Codex Sinaiticus).
[3]E.g., Mark 10:46ff.

Such a problem immediately stimulates the very human speculation among Christ's disciples about the cause of the situation: who is to blame? They enumerate the possibilities: first, they wonder if the man himself is to blame, but realizing the absurdity of this (for how could he sin before birth?), they decide that his parents are to blame instead. But Christ quickly dispenses with their speculations and states that the blind man's malformation happened "that the works of God may be manifest in him" (Jn 9.3). The Blessed Theophylact (eleventh century) in his commentary on St John's Gospel makes the important observation that the conjunction translated as "that" (*hina*, Greek) in verse 3 is "often used to express the outcome, but not the intended result, of the action stated in the main clause."[4] Thus, "Jesus' words here ... do not supply the reason why the man was born blind, but state the consequence – good came from evil, to the glory of God."[5] It was not St John's purpose to give an explanation for the presence of sin and suffering in the world, but rather to demonstrate the divinity of Jesus Christ. Only the Creator can complete and finish an incomplete creation, even to the point of using the dust of the ground, as in the first creation, that has been moistened and vivified by the touch of divine saliva. Theophylact places this sign in the context of the events immediately preceding the encounter with the man born blind, events in which Christ was nearly stoned for making himself equal to God (Jn 8.58–59): "It is clear that Christ performed this miracle as God Who is before Abraham. To prove this to the Jews, He intentionally approached the blind man, and not vice versa."[6]

St Irenaeus (second century) interprets "that the *works* of God may be manifest in him" as a direct reference to the continuing work of God as Creator of the human person:

Now the work of God is the fashioning of man. For, as the Scripture says, He made [man] by a kind of process: "And the Lord took clay

[4]Blessed Theophylact, *The Explanation of the Holy Gospel According to John*, trans. Fr Christopher Stade (House Springs, MO: Chrysostom Press, 2007), 152.
[5]Ibid.
[6]Ibid., 150.

from the earth, and formed man." Wherefore also the Lord spat on the ground and made clay, and smeared it upon the eyes, pointing out the original fashioning [of man], how it was effected, and manifesting the hand of God to those who can understand by what [hand] man was formed out of the dust. For that which the artificer, the Word, had omitted to form in the womb [viz., the blind man's eyes], He then supplied in public, that the works of God might be manifested in him, in order that we might not be seeking out another hand by which man was fashioned, nor another Father; knowing that this hand of God which formed us at the beginning, and which does form us in the womb, has in these last times sought us out who were lost, winning back His own, and taking up the lost sheep upon His shoulders, and with joy restoring it to the fold of life. . . . As, therefore, we are by the Word formed in the womb, this very same Word formed the visual power in him who had been blind from his birth; showing openly who it is that fashions us in secret, since the Word Himself had been made manifest to men: and declaring the original formation of Adam, and the manner in which he was created, and by what hand he was fashioned, *indicating the whole from a part* [emphasis added]. For the Lord who formed the visual powers, is He who made the whole man, carrying out the will of the Father.[7]

In this remarkable miracle, Christ fully demonstrates who he is, the Word of God who created man in the beginning. The man born blind is a type of the failed human creation, which through the fall acquired blindness in its relationship with the divine. The Word made flesh comes to restore, complete, and heal the earlier creation that failed through disobedience. Christ not only fashions new and healthy eyes to restore vision to his creature, but also illuminates those eyes by sending the blind man to wash them through a type of baptism so that they may become the means of a deeper enlightenment:

---

[7]Irenaeus, *Against Heresies* 5.15.2–3 (ANF 1:543).

And inasmuch as man . . . having fallen into transgression, needed the laver of regeneration, [the Lord] said to him [upon whom He had conferred sight], after He had smeared his eyes with the clay, "Go to Siloam, and wash;" thus restoring to him both [his perfect] confirmation, and that regeneration which takes place by means of the laver. And for this reason when he was washed he came seeing, that he might both know Him who had fashioned him, and that man might learn [to know] Him who has conferred upon him life.[8]

Through this single sign, Christ vividly demonstrates by tangible means his mission as the incarnate Word of God. He comes to heal and complete a creation, which through disobedience has sundered its connection to the Source of life. In fashioning perfect eyes for the man born blind, the Lord creates the possibility not only of physical sight in his creature, but also of spiritual vision, opening the way through faith to a healing knowledge of the invisible and unknowable God. The healing of the man born blind is an icon of the mystery of baptism, which the Church has called illumination. By obeying the command to go and wash the mud that has touched his face, the man born blind begins a journey of faith that is a progressive ascent toward an ever-deeper encounter with the living God that begins with all the senses, but ultimately transcends them.

While the man born blind makes his ascent toward God, the Pharisees, who have no sensory impediment, descend into an irremediable blindness through envy and pride. Rather than acknowledge the extraordinary nature of the sign of which they are witnesses, they seek to discredit the One who has done the unprecedented by condemning him as a sinner for performing the miracle on the Sabbath. They refuse to see that the very Person who can complete that which was not completed in the womb is the One who also continues without temporal interruption to guide the creative process of development for every child in the womb. The terrible irony is that excellent visual acuity in

[8]Ibid.

no way guarantees clear vision. The passions, especially pride, become filters that distort our interpretation of reality. Even if we can describe with great accuracy shapes and colors that we observe with our sense of sight, our interpretation of what we see may lead us to conclusions that are far divergent from the perceptions of the physically blind who yet "see" through the lens of humility.

The healing of the man born blind highlights an essential and very practical implication of the incarnation. God is pure spirit. But when God the Word united himself with his material creation, the spiritual acquired materiality, and conversely, the material was infused with the spiritual. This truth is at the heart of the lived experience of the mysteries of the Church. The mysteries or sacraments of the Church (e.g., baptism, marriage, confession, anointing the sick, the Eucharist) all represent the strongest evidence that the life in Christ embraces everything, and that embrace begins through material means. Physical elements are central to all of the mysteries. They make it possible for each believer to be literally touched by the divine, the spiritual reality hidden within the physical elements of the mystery. Thus, for example, each believer is illuminated through washing with the waters of baptism, just as the man born blind was illuminated after washing with the waters of Siloam. The early Christians were not only enjoined to pray for the sick, but also the presbyters of the Church were called to anoint the sick person with oil in the name of the Lord (Jas 5.14). It is the wedding of tangible, material means with the spiritual that forms the prayer of faith that heals/saves[9] the sick person.

Let us return to the beginning of chapter 9 of St John's Gospel to reflect on one other aspect of the account of the healing of the man born blind. It was noted that in some very early texts there is a variant reading of verse 4: "*We* [rather than *I*] must perform the works of the One who sent me, while it is day; for night is coming when no one will be able to work." This variant reading emphasizes the shared nature of Christ's work in the world. With a sense of urgency ("while it is day"), he is urging his followers to also "perform the works of the One who

[9]The Greek *sōsei* has the double meaning of salvation and healing in James 5.15.

sent me." When considering the meaning of the healing of the man who had been born blind for the sacramental life of the Church, what is the significance of the "we" versus "I" of other textual variants? Could not this emphasis on the first-person plural refer to the Church's ongoing sacramental ministry, which Christ established before his ascension? But then, what is the significance of his qualifying statement about performing the works "while it is day"? St John Chrysostom has provided a very thoughtful analysis of this passage in which he has emphasized the importance of the difference between Christ's uses of the imagery of day and night:

> "While it is day, while men may believe on Me, while this life lasteth, I must work. The night cometh," that is, futurity [the future], "when no man can work." He said not, "when I cannot work," but, "when no man can work:" that is, when there is no longer faith, nor labors, nor repentance. For to show that He calleth faith, a "work," when they say unto Him, "What shall we do, that we might work the works of God?" (e.g., John 6:28), He replieth, "This is the work of God, that ye believe on Him whom He hath sent." How then can no man work this work in the future world? Because there faith is not, but all, willingly, or unwillingly, will submit.[10]

It is in this life, then, where the exercise of faith is possible and so crucial. The healing of the man born blind underscores the very strong bond between faith and the senses, especially the sense of touch, when the blind man experienced the application to his face of the dust transformed by the saliva of the Word made flesh. Unquestioning, humble obedience resulted in his going to the pool of Siloam and washing, both of which were acts of faith, unimpeded by reason and rationalization. After feeling the initial splashes of water, physical light began to dawn, with spiritual illumination closely following. Thus, the foundation of this sign of Christ's divinity was touch—the loving touch of the Creator, who would become a creature to touch, heal, and thereby re-create his creature.

[10]St John Chrysostom, *Homilies on St John* 56.2 (NPNF[1] 14:202).

THE HEALING OF THE WOMAN
WITH AN ISSUE OF BLOOD

ΙϹ ΧϹ

Plate 5

CHAPTER 4

The Touch of Faith

Few are they who by faith touch him; multitudes are they who throng about him. —St Augustine[1]

And, behold, one of the rulers of the synagogue, whose name was Jairus, seeing him, fell at his feet, and begged him greatly, saying, "My little daughter is dying. Come and lay your hands on her, that she may be healed and live." And he went with him. A great crowd followed and pressed upon him. A woman who had had a hemorrhage for twelve years, and who had suffered much from many physicians, having spent all that she had, received no benefit, but rather grew worse. Hearing about Jesus, she came in the crowd behind, and touched his garment. For she said, "If I just touch his clothes, I shall be healed." And immediately her hemorrhage stopped, and she sensed in her body that she was healed from her torment. And Jesus, immediately knowing in himself that power had gone out of him, turned around in the crowd and said, "Who touched my clothes?" And his disciples said unto him, "You see the crowd pressing upon you, and you say, 'Who touched me?'" But he looked round about to see her who had done this thing. The woman, knowing what had happened to her, with fear and trembling, came and fell down before him and told him all the truth. And he said to her, "Daughter, your faith has saved you; go in peace and be healed and freed from your torment." —Mark 5.22–24 (author's translation)

S<small>T AUGUSTINE</small> makes a crucial distinction between Jesus' being "pressed upon" (*synthlibō*, Greek)[2] and the touch (*haptō*, Greek) of faith by the woman with the chronic hemorrhage. Whereas the

---

[1] St Augustine, Sermon 62.4, in ACCS:NT 2:75.
[2] In St Luke's Gospel (8.42), another Greek word, *sympnigō*, which can be translated

action of the many in the crowd was random and reflected no clear intentions, the action of the woman was of a distinctly different character. The healing of the woman with the chronic hemorrhage presents a striking contrast to the healing of the man born blind described in the ninth chapter of St John's Gospel. As can be seen in plate 5, the woman approaches Christ by stealth from behind and touches just the edge or fringe (*kraspedon*, Greek) of his garment (as noted in the Gospels of Sts Matthew and Luke), reasoning in herself that making indirect contact with Christ by merely touching that which touches him, his clothing, will be sufficient for her to receive healing.

With the man born blind, Christ reveals himself as Creator in the very public act of applying the mud to the man's malformed eyes, while, with the woman with a hemorrhage, his divinity is revealed when she approaches him in stealth with faith: "Using a woman whom they could see, he enabled them to see the divinity that cannot be seen. The Son's divinity became known through his healing, and the afflicted woman's faith was revealed through her being healed."[3] In both instances, touch is a critical factor in the revelation of the incarnate Word of God.

The reality of the incarnation makes it possible for God to make intimate contact with his wounded creation, both by his own intentional, active touch—as with the man born blind—and also by his passively receiving the touch of faith from his creature in the person of this woman, who had suffered so long. It is precisely the reciprocal character of touch in both its active and passive aspects which, in material terms, underlies the reality of every mystery of the faith.[4] The mysteries, or sacraments, all utilize physical means to make possible this mutual exchange, an exchange that is the foundation of the healing relationship. Thus, the absolute trust of the one seeking healing and the infinite compassion of the Healer meet through the medium of touch. It is not

as "crowd around, press upon" or even "crush," is used to emphasize the multiple close physical contacts between Christ and others in the crowd.

[3] St Ephrem the Syrian, *Commentary on Tatian's Diatessaron* 7.1–2, in ACCS: NT 3: 144.

[4] This tension between the passive and active aspects of touch is even reflected in the use of the middle voice of the Greek verb *haptō* to convey its meaning.

uncommon to say that one has been touched by an act of kindness or by witnessing the poignant nature of another's sorrow or suffering. It is not difficult then to see that touch, in either its physical or metaphorical manifestation, is at the heart of the encounter between persons.

A striking feature of this particular healing encounter was the explicit exchange of energies between the two participants that is described in the gospel accounts. It is as if a light has briefly illuminated a phenomenon that in so many other miracles of Christ's healing ministry remained shrouded in mystery. The release of power from Christ to this woman was a foretaste of what was to come after Pentecost when he had gone to the Father. "Truly, truly, I tell you, the one who believes in me shall do the works that I do, indeed he shall do greater than these because I go to the Father" (Jn 14.12, author's translation). Thus, it should not be surprising that even the Apostle Peter's shadow falling upon and touching the sick (Acts 5.15) or contact with relics of the saints could release the power of the Holy Spirit and bring healing. Buried deep within this exchange between Christ and the woman is another Theophany, revealing not only Christ's divinity, but also the indwelling of the Holy Spirit within the God-Man, the promise of which would become manifest in the lives and actions of the saints following the descent of the fire of Pentecost. In his defense of the divinity of the Holy Spirit, St John Chrysostom cites the transformation wrought in the apostles, including St Peter, after Pentecost:

> For had they not borne a King's image and their radiancy been unapproachable, their garments and shadows had not wrought so mightily. For the garments of a king are terrible even to robbers. Wouldst thou see this beaming even through the body? "Looking steadfastly," said he, "upon the face of Stephen, they saw it as the face of an angel." (Acts 6:15) But this was nothing to the glory flashing within.[5]

The woman's act of faith is reflected in the popular piety of some Orthodox Christian churches or jurisdictions, in which, during the

[5]St John Chrysostom, *Homily 7 on Second Corinthians* (NPNF[1] 12:314).

healing or unction service, not only do the faithful touch the fringe of the priest's stole (*epitrachēlion*, Greek) during the prayers, but also those who cannot be in direct contact with the *epitrachēlion* create a chain of contact in faith through touching those who are in contact. Thus, the touch of faith can be a shared communal act, another form of the communion that occurs most profoundly in the shared celebration of the Eucharist from the common cup.

The Fathers of the Church make a point of emphasizing the juxtaposition of this miracle with the raising of Jairus's daughter. They contrast the apparently weaker faith of Jairus, as representative of the Jewish nation, who begged Christ to come and lay his hands on his daughter, with that of the woman who was firmly convinced that healing would come even through the indirect, furtive touch of his clothing. When in humility she approached Christ from behind, she is presented as a type of the Gentiles, not unlike the Centurion who stated his unworthiness to have Christ come under his roof—"Only say the word"—when he asked for the healing of his servant (Lk 7.6ff.). St Ephrem emphasizes how the woman gave her divine Healer the proper honor in the way she approached him, and how he, in turn, honored her deep faith by exposing her to the crowd: "This is why he cried out, 'Who touched my garments?' He said this so that all the people might know who touched *more* than anyone else did. She chose to honor him more than others do, first, by approaching from behind, and second, in that she touched the fringe of his cloak."[6]

What constitutes the *more* of her touching in comparison to the jostling of Christ by the crowd? In other words, what was unique about this woman's touch of Christ's clothing? Recent research studies in the neurophysiology of touch using functional magnetic resonance imaging may give some additional insight into the *more* associated with the suffering woman's touch. These studies have highlighted the complex role of multiple sites in the brain in the perception and interpretation of

---

[6]St Ephrem the Syrian, *Commentary on Tatian's Diatessaron* 7.10, in ACCS:NT 3:145 (emphasis added).

Color Plates

Icons from the
Dormition of the Mother of God Monastery
(Rives Junction, Michigan)

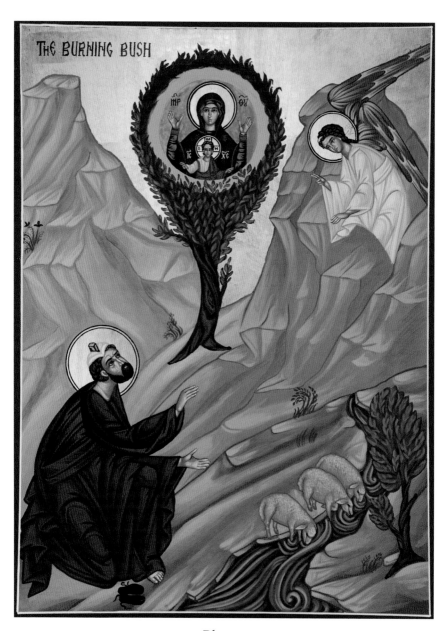

Plate 1

Plate 2

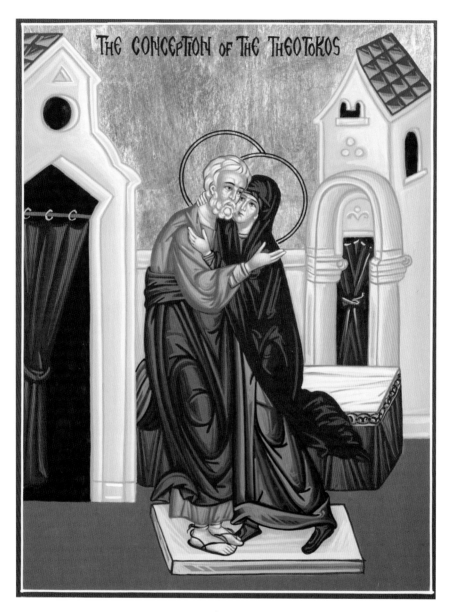

Plate 3

Plate 4

Plate 5

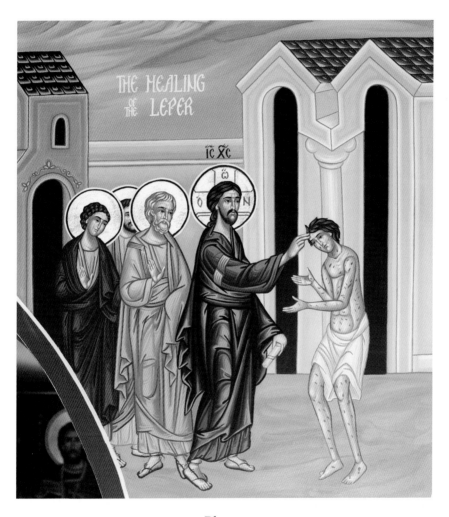

Plate 6

Plate 7

Plate 8

Plate 9

Plate 10

Plate 11

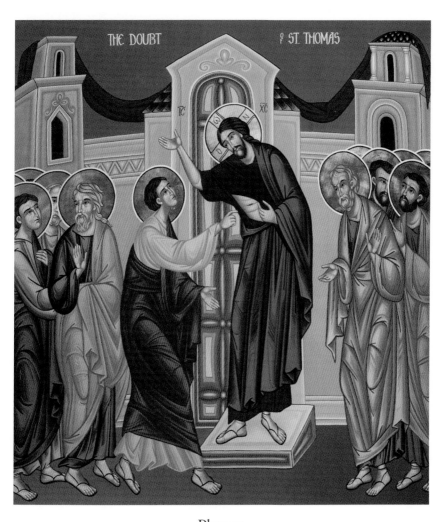

Plate 12

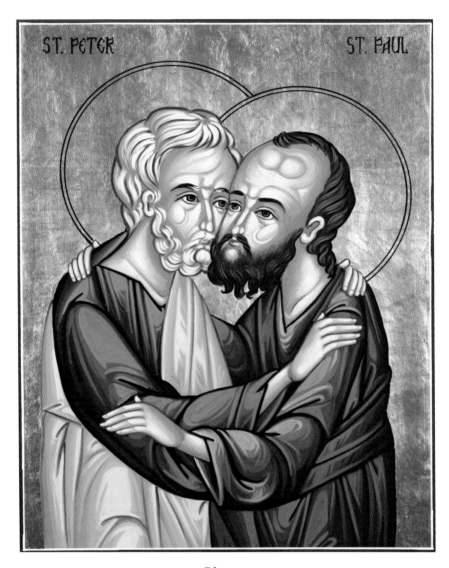

ST. PETER   ST. PAUL

Plate 13

Plate 14

a tactile stimulus.[7] Fundamentally, the intentional nature of touch is to a major degree defined by its being an emotional or affective experience. There are parts of the cortex of the brain (where higher brain functions occur) that facilitate the affective experience of tactile stimuli as positive or pleasant; negative or unpleasant; and neutral, neither pleasant nor unpleasant. Neutral (nonaffective) tactile stimuli are processed in a distinctly different part of the cortex than those tactile stimuli that have affective elements. Although pleasant and unpleasant tactile stimuli are processed in some of the same regions of the cortex, they exhibit patterns that are unique for each.[8] A striking example of this connection between affect and meaning in touch has been shown in a study of the cortical processing of a tactile stimulus to the forearm of subjects, in the form of skin cream being rubbed on the skin. The use of the descriptors "rich moisturizing cream" versus "basic cream" for the exact same substance had a significant impact on how the stimulus was perceived at the cortical level,[9] with the subjects receiving the "rich moisturizing cream" experiencing greater pleasantness from the experience. So it seems that affect, meaning, and, by extension, intent are interconnected. Thus, it can be appreciated that the *more* of the woman's touch reflected the powerful effect of accumulated emotion and meaning generated over years of suffering that was lacking in the others in the crowd, who were merely jostling Christ. All of this intense energy was released in the touch she gave to the fringe of Christ's clothing when she said to herself, *If I just touch his clothes, I shall be healed.* Watered by trust, the seed of faith rapidly germinated as she reached out to touch his clothing. Compared to the random contacts of the crowd with Christ, her touch was indeed much more than any other contact he received during his journey to raise Jairus' daughter.

[7]For an excellent review, see E. T. Rolls, "The Affective and Cognitive Processing of Touch, Oral Texture, and Temperature in the Brain," *Neuroscience and Biobehavioral Reviews* 34 (2010): 237–45.

[8]Ibid.

[9]C. McCabe, E. T. Rolls, A. Bilderbeck, and F. McGlone, "Cognitive Influences on the Affective Representation of Touch and the Sight of Touch in the Human Brain," *Social Cognitive and Affective Neuroscience* 3 (2008): 97–108.

How is it possible that the woman could know instantly that her hemorrhage had stopped? The precise cause of her chronic bleeding is unknown, but it is probable that the source of her bleeding was associated with intense physical pain. Instantaneous relief of pain associated with elimination of the underlying cause of her chronic bleeding could have been the likely herald of her cure rather than the more indistinct cessation of a chronic hemorrhage. Pressure exerted by a large uterine (arising from the womb) tumor (e.g., a leiomyoma)[10] that had also ulcerated might account for her severe physical distress and the chronic bleeding.

It is also important to reflect on the nature of this woman's torment and her terrible suffering (*mastix*, Greek).[11] Dame Cicely Saunders, the founder of the modern hospice movement, developed the concept of *total pain* to capture the totality of distress that constitutes human suffering.[12] She identified at least four dimensions in which the human person experiences distress: physical, psychological, social, and spiritual. The woman with the chronic hemorrhage is a prime example of the phenomenon of *total pain*. The Gospel accounts mention not only her intense physical distress, but also convey indirectly the other dimensions of her suffering. She could not approach Christ openly, because her continuous hemorrhage made her and anyone with whom she came in contact ritually unclean (Lev 15.25–27). Ritual uncleanness had been a way of life for her during the previous twelve years, making her the equivalent of a leper, shunned by family, friends, and community. Her sense of profound isolation produced intense psychological as well as social pain. Whereas the persistent evidence of her ritual uncleanness, which separated her from the community, would visibly and tangibly be present in the form of the blood oozing into her clothing, the inner pain associated with the bleeding would be invisible

[10] A not-uncommon form of benign tumor arising from the muscle in the wall of the uterus that can be multiple and that, over time, can achieve large dimensions.

[11] This Greek word literally refers to beatings and whippings, i.e., torture. Thus, metaphorically it conveys the intensity of the truly horrible suffering of this woman.

[12] D. Clark, "'Total pain,' disciplinary power and the body in the work of Cicely Saunders, 1958–1967," *Social Science & Medicine* 49 (1999): 727–36.

to others and remain an added private torment, making her psychological distress even more excruciating. Her social distress was magnified, as was her physical pain, by the repeated and expensive failures of her physicians to cure her condition. The combination of these three forms of persistent suffering, especially in light of the apparently hopeless nature of her condition, would inevitably tempt her toward despair and to great spiritual distress, perhaps even to a feeling of being abandoned and cursed by God. The power that emanated from Christ in response to her touch of faith and hope touched all four dimensions of her suffering, not only immediately stopping the hemorrhage, but also bringing her to real health in a new relationship with the Source of health, so that Christ could add his benediction, "Go in peace," summing up the full nature of her healing.

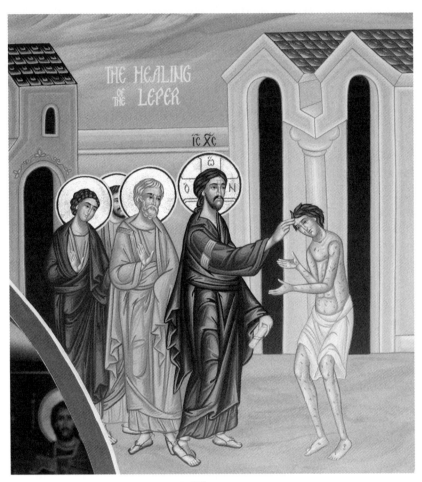

Plate 6

CHAPTER 5

Touching Death

And the leper who has the disease, his garments shall be undone, his head shall be exposed, and he shall cover his mouth and cry, "Unclean!"
—Lev 13.45, LXX[1]

And it happened while he was in one of the towns, behold, there was a man full of leprosy who upon seeing Jesus fell on his face and implored him, saying, "Lord, if you will, you can make me clean." Extending his hand, he touched him, saying, "I will; be clean." And immediately the leprosy left him. He told him, "Tell no one, but rather, go and show yourself to the priest and make an offering for your cleansing, just as Moses commanded, as a witness to them."
—Luke 5.12–14, author's translation

THE PHENOMENON OF TOUCH is quite complex; it embraces a range of sensations, including the ability to sense textures (hard, soft, rough, smooth), apparent weight or pressure (light or heavy), temperature (hot, neutral, cold), and pain or pleasure.[2] Because the skin is flexible and not rigid, touch of various kinds produces indentation or deformation of the skin. The speed, intensity, and force with which a stimulus interacts with the sensory receptors (mechanoreceptors) in the skin determine how the stimulus is perceived: for example, as gentle stroking, pressure, or painful compression. Temperature and pain sensors add additional levels of perception, and higher cognitive processing

[1] The Greek word translated as "disease" in Leviticus 13.45 LXX, *hē haphē*, ironically also means the sense of touch; thus the disease of leprosy was already understood in ancient times to be a communicable disease, thought to be acquired by contact with the afflicted.

[2] For an excellent review, see E. P. Gardner, "Touch," *Encyclopedia of Life Sciences* (Chichester, UK: John Wiley and Sons, May 2010), 1–12.

of tactile stimuli can further define the affective or emotional aspects of the experience as pleasant, neutral, or unpleasant.

It is the sense of touch, which is so critical for orienting human beings within their environment, that creates a sense of self. The highest concentrations of the many specialized mechanoreceptors that sense a variety of subtle forms of touch are in the fingertips. For example, these receptors make it possible for a blind person to discriminate between the individual raised dots of the Braille system, which are later integrated at the cortical level, as meaningful patterns of dots so that reading through one's fingers can occur. Loss of the complex sensory functions in the hand that provide continual feedback to higher command centers in the brain can produce severely impaired function. The ability to sense external stimuli that are painful to touch is part of the homeostatic mechanisms that protect the organism from harm.[3]

Leprosy, an infectious disease caused by the bacterium *Mycobacterium leprae*, is an ancient scourge of the human race. The bacteria thrive in cooler, more peripheral portions of the body and reside within inflammatory cells (macrophages) and Schwann cells that make up the sheaths of peripheral sensory nerves. The disease has a range of manifestations, from milder to more destructive forms, manifestations that are mirrored in the amount of tissue loss and are dependent on the immune response of the infected host. Although the peripheral neuropathy (nerve injury) produced by the infection can cause loss of sensation and numbness, leading to inadvertent tissue injury and destruction, severe pain can, ironically, also be a feature of the illness associated with partially damaged nerves.[4] By virtue of the unique targets of the mycobacteria causing the disease, lepers lose sensory connection with the peripheral portions of their extremities and face as their disease progresses. Their flesh begins to disintegrate, and they prematurely experience the isolation of the dying. The raw, diseased,

---

[3] A. D. Craig, "A new view of pain as a homeostatic emotion," *Trends in Neurosciences* 26.6 (2003): 303–7.

[4] S. Thakur, R. H. Dworkin, O. M. O. Haroun, D. N. J. Lockwood, and A. S. C. Rice, "Acute and chronic pain associated with leprosy," *Pain* 156 (2015): 998–1002.

and necrotic flesh coexists with the living, representing a visible, tangible, and stinking reminder of their mortality.

It was a bold act on the part of the leper to approach Christ (see plate 6). Whereas the uncleanness and ritual impurity of the woman with the chronic hemorrhage were probably not immediately recognizable, the impurity of this walking corpse would have been obvious to everyone in the crowd, who would definitely be inclined to flee as he approached. After all, the Levitical rules were clear. He would have been instructed to keep his defilement visible for all to see and avoid, while also being required to announce his presence by shouting, "Unclean!" just in case someone was so unfortunate as to not see him coming (Lev 13.45). And yet, he still approaches Christ, who does not shrink from his approach.

The Church fathers commend the great faith of the leper, who in his request acknowledges Christ's divinity. As St John Chrysostom emphasizes, "For neither did he say [to Christ], 'If Thou request it of God,' nor, 'If Thou pray,' but, 'If *Thou wilt*, Thou canst make me clean.' Nor did he say, 'Lord, cleanse me,' but leaves all to Him, and makes his recovery depend on Him, and testifies that all the authority is His."[5] The leper's deep faith in Christ is manifest in a relationship of complete trust and humble acceptance of whatever Christ wills for him. Christ's attitude toward the leper and his condition are in marked contrast to that of the Prophet Elisha, who naturally dreads to be in proximity to the unclean leper Naaman (4 Kgdms [2 Kgs] 5.12). As the Blessed Theophylact (eleventh century) states in his commentary on the Gospel according to St Mark, "Remember that Elisha had such reverence for the law that he could not endure to see, let alone touch, Naaman who was a leper asking for healing."[6] However, the Word-made-flesh, who originally directed Moses concerning the treatment of lepers, now demonstrates his authority over the same law by superseding it through his touch and healing contact with the leper. St John Chrysostom highlights the

[5] St John Chrysostom, *Homily 25 on the Gospel of St Matthew* (NPNF[1] 10:172) (emphasis added).

[6] Blessed Theophylact, *Explanation of the Holy Gospel According to Mark*, 22.

unique character of Christ's declaration in his dialogue with the leper of his willingness to make him clean. In contrast to the apostles' disavowals regarding healings wrought through them in the early Church (Acts 3.12) and his own modesty, in this instance by saying, "I will," Christ explicitly confirms his authority as God to heal the leper:

> But the Lord, though He spake oftentimes many things modestly, and beneath His own glory, what saith He here, to establish the doctrine of them that were amazed at Him for His authority? "I will, be thou clean." Although in the many and great signs which He wrought, He nowhere appears to have uttered this word. Here however, to confirm the surmise both of all the people and of the leper touching His authority, He purposely added, "I will."[7]

But, why did Christ, who could heal with a word, proceed to touch the leper? St John in his commentary illuminates an essential feature of what might otherwise seem like a superfluous act by Christ in this miracle:

> But He did not merely say, "I will, be thou clean," but He also, "put forth His hand, and touched him;" a thing especially worthy of inquiry. For wherefore, when cleansing him by will and word, did He add also the touch of His hand? It seems to me, for no other end, but that, He might signify by this also, that He is not subject to the law, but is set over it; and that to the clean, henceforth, nothing is unclean.[8]

Returning to the striking contrast between the prophet Elisha's treatment of the leper Naaman and Christ's encounter with the leper, St John adds,

> For this cause, we see, Elisha did not so much as see Naaman, but though he perceived he was offended at his not coming out and touching him, observing the strictness of the law, he abides at home,

---

[7] St John Chrysostom, *Homily 25 on Matthew* (NPNF[1] 10:172).
[8] Ibid., NPNF[1] 10:173.

and sends him to Jordan to wash. Whereas the Lord, to signify that
He heals not as a servant, but as absolute master, doth also touch.
For His hand became not unclean from the leprosy, but the leprous
body was rendered clean by His holy hand.[9]

The healing of the leper in many ways recapitulates and extends
the sign given by Christ's healing of the man born blind (Jn 9.1ff.). By
healing the man born blind, Christ demonstrates as Creator his ability
to complete and finish an incomplete creation. In the case of the leper,
he demonstrates his ability as God to heal and restore a damaged and
corrupted creation. Indeed, his encounter and intentional touch of the
leper is the beginning of an ever-increasing series of confrontations
between the God-Man and the decay inherent in human suffering
and mortality. Beginning with the leper, Christ, through his humanity,
touches, and through his divinity, reverses, the marks of corruption to
which human flesh is subject—marks that have progressively isolated
suffering humanity in its broken state. By his touch, Christ reverses all
of this and restores the leper's full participation in the land of the living.
He is not only ritually *clean* before his fellow Jews, but also purified and
cleansed before God. His physical healing is only the beginning. The
concomitant psychological, social, and spiritual isolation and distress,
which have haunted his existence, are immediately destroyed through
the divine-human touch of the incarnate Lord. Now with his sense of
touch restored, the leper can become reoriented to the cosmos, finding
his way back from exile to renewed relationships with God and his fellow creatures. From divine mercy and condescension to human need,
Christ instructs him to show himself to the priest and offer the prescribed sacrifice so that he will be fully reconciled under the law to others in his community, even though the effect of Christ's touch has far
transcended the power and dictates of the law. Indeed, the holy fathers
have observed that the offering required for a healed leper prescribed
in Leviticus (13.8) was a type of the sacrificial death of Christ for the
healing of leprous humanity tainted by sin and death:

[9]Ibid.

We may see, then, in the birds (offered at the cleansing of the leper) Christ suffering in the flesh according to the Scriptures but remaining also beyond the power of suffering. . . . That the one bird then was slain, and that the other was baptized indeed in its blood, while itself exempt from slaughter, typified what was really to happen. For Christ died in our place, and we, who have been baptized into his death, he has saved by his own blood.[10]

The Blessed Theophylact, in his commentary on the Gospel according to St Luke, further illuminates the deeper meaning of the metaphor within the sacrifice: "The two birds are the two natures of Christ, the divine and the human, one of which was slain, namely His human nature, while the other was released, alive. The divine nature remained unsuffering, but it was anointed with the blood of the suffering nature, taking upon itself that suffering."[11]

By virtue of the incarnate Lord's transformation of touch, he provided an example for all Christians as well as a means by which he continues to tangibly heal through the presence of the Holy Spirit in the members of his body. Early Christians were noted for their fearlessness in the face of death as they cared for the sick and dying during great epidemics.[12] St Basil the Great, archbishop of Caesarea in Cappadocia (+379), took this directly to heart and, by following his Master's example, transformed the care of lepers within the Christian Roman Empire.[13] It was the unhesitating willingness of the compassionate physician-archbishop to personally touch dying lepers as he cared for and comforted them in his *kelyphokomeion*, a prototype of hospice, that astounded his contemporaries. By touching the leper, Christ demonstrated the divine intention to touch and thereby cleanse his unclean,

---

[10]St Cyril of Alexandria, *Commentary on Luke*, Homily 12, in ACCS:NT 3:91.

[11]Blessed Theophylact, *Explanation of the Holy Gospel According to Luke*, 59.

[12]Eusebius, *Ecclesiastical History*, vol. 2, LCL 265:185–87.

[13]St Gregory of Nazianzus, *Oration, Panegyric on St Basil* 43.63 (NPNF² 7:416). For a more detailed review of early Christian attitudes to the sick and St Basil's care of lepers, also see Daniel B. Hinshaw, *Suffering and the Nature of Healing* (Yonkers, NY: St Vladimir's Seminary Press, 2013), 24–28.

broken, and decaying creation, not unlike the command to Moses at the burning bush to remove his sandals, which served as barriers between the human and the divine. Saints like Basil of Caesarea followed the Lord's example, recognizing that in their embrace of suffering, decaying humanity, a deeper invisible healing is transmitted.

Christ's healing encounter with the leper was one of the earliest signs of his mastery over the corruption caused by human sin and mortality. The raising of Lazarus, who had begun to experience decomposition by the fourth day in the tomb, was, by extension, a further demonstration of his power as God over the ravages of time and decay. Both of these miracles were, in turn, signs pointing to his ultimate conquest of this central defining aspect of fallen humanity by his full embrace and destruction of death through his own crucifixion, death, and resurrection. In saying, "I will," to the leper, he expressed the fullness of love within the Holy Trinity. By touching death in the leper, he demonstrated the transformation of will into action, making touch offered in love a healing mystery of his kingdom.

THE BAPTISM   ℈ OUR LORD

IC XC

Plate 7

CHAPTER 6

Touching the Cosmos

And it happened that while all the people were being baptized, Jesus was also baptized, and as he prayed, heaven was opened and he saw the Holy Spirit descend upon him in bodily form as a dove, and a voice from heaven came: "You are my beloved Son, in whom I am well pleased."

—Luke 3.21–22, author's translation

THE SYNOPTIC GOSPELS present different details about the baptism of Christ. St Matthew emphasizes St John the Baptist's reluctance to baptize Jesus, as St John declares rather his need to be baptized by Jesus, and Christ in turn reassures him that he should proceed, for "it is fitting for us to fulfill all righteousness" (Mt 3.15). St Mark, like St Matthew, provides the additional information that the site of the baptism was the Jordan River and that John baptized Jesus (Mk 1.9). What all three accounts agree upon is most tersely stated in St Luke's Gospel: the heavens opening, the dove descending upon Christ, and the voice declaring him to be "my beloved Son." Interestingly, St Mark diverges from the two other evangelists in using the Greek word *schizō* to describe in more dramatic language the "splitting" or "tearing open" of the heavens, in contrast to the Greek word *anoigō*, translated as "open," that is used in the other accounts—perhaps to emphasize the unprecedented nature of the event.

In the theophany there is an unbroken chain of touch descending from the Father, who touches his Son by sending the Holy Spirit as a dove to alight upon him. Through the Son the Father touches the entire creation in Christ's baptism in the Jordan River (see plate 7), acknowledging him as his Son through the resounding touch of his voice. What had happened in secret with the coming of the Holy Spirit to the Virgin Mary at the annunciation is now recapitulated and publically acknowledged at the Jordan River.

It is no accident that God the Holy Trinity touched us through water. Water is the sine qua non of our biological, created existence. By virtue of the ongoing cycle of evaporation, movement in clouds, and condensation in a variety of forms as rain, snow, sleet, or even hail, water can touch every portion of our planet. The water sanctified by contact with the Son of God has in some very real sense extended St John's action in the Jordan River to a baptism of the whole created order of this fallen and suffering world. The second-century Church father St Hippolytus emphasized the healing nature of the divine contact with water, through which God has been reconciled with his entire creation:

> Do you see, beloved, how many and how great blessings we would have lost if the Lord had yielded to the exhortation of John and declined baptism? For the heavens had been shut before this. The region above was inaccessible. We might descend to the lower parts, but not ascend to the upper. So it happened not only that the Lord was being baptized—he also was making new the old creation. He was bringing the alienated under the scepter of adoption. For straightway, "the heavens were opened to him." A reconciliation took place between the visible and the invisible. The celestial orders were filled with joy, the diseases of earth were healed, secret things made known, those at enmity restored to amity.[1]

Thus, Christ, in reference to his own humble insistence on being baptized by St John the Baptist—"It is fitting for us to fulfill all righteousness"—expanded the meaning of the mystery of baptism to include his restoration of everything in creation to its proper state: *to fulfill all righteousness*. He does this by prefiguring his own salvific death, burial, and resurrection via his humble submersion in the baptismal waters of the Jordan River. Through this essential, life-giving, and omnipresent liquid, he touches all the living, including those yet to be

---

[1] St Hippolytus, *The Discourse on the Holy Theophany* 106 (ANF 5:236).

born, transcending time and place. The metaphor extends beyond the individual to collectively embrace all of the creation, all that is touched by this most extraordinary of solvents; even the inanimate is washed in the mystery of his touch extended through the medium of water.

The early Fathers of the Church saw very distinct parallels between the violent destruction of the earth in Noah's flood and the subsequent baptism of all Christians in the baptism of Christ. Death and resurrection are the central meanings of both Noah's flood as type and Christian baptism as its antitype (1 Pet 3.21). Just as a righteous God washes away the evil of a fallen world in the ancient flood, so Christ—*to fulfill all righteousness*—is baptized in the Jordan, providing not only the antitype of Noah's flood but also instituting the type of his death and resurrection by which his broken creation is washed and re-created. Water remains the metaphor that links all together. Characteristic of the fundamental paradox underlying the Christian faith, this extraordinary metaphor of transcendent life cannot be separated from destruction and death. Indeed, it is the baptismal death and resurrection of the entire cosmos, initiated by Christ's contact with the waters of the Jordan River, that fulfill all righteousness. Just as the crucified Lord rests on the seventh day, the great and holy Sabbath, and is raised as the new Adam on the eighth day, so also eight persons passed through the death and destruction of the ancient flood and were saved. St Jerome identifies Noah's ark with the Church: "Noah's ark was a type of the Church, as the Apostle Peter says—'In Noah's ark few, that is, eight souls, were saved through water: which also after a true likeness doth now save us, even baptism'" [1 Pet 3.20–21].[2]

In a very real sense, the Holy Trinity touched the entire creation at the Theophany when Christ was baptized in the Jordan River. As opposed to the violent abruptness and destruction of Noah's flood, his touch was a healing of a different and subtler kind, one that was set in motion at the Jordan and continues "until the end of the age" (cf. Mt 28.10). Not unlike the encounter of St Elias (Elijah) with God in the still small voice on Mt Horeb (1 Kgs 19.10ff.), the revelatory power of

[2]St Jerome, *The Dialogue against the Luciferians* 22 (NPNF[2] 6:331).

Christ's baptism was hidden in his humility in accepting baptism. In touching the material creation in so direct and yet gentle a manner, the new Adam invites all who unite themselves to him through baptism to cooperate—even to participate—with him in the healing of the cosmos. This cooperation must be voluntary and grounded in the realization that all who choose to cooperate with the divine in the healing of creation are, in microcosm, realizing the fullness of that same healing within themselves, for each human creature is a *microcosmos*, capable, by grace, of union with the Source of that healing touch. And if we are united to the Source, we have the rest: all of creation, the communion of the saints, and the holy angels—an entire universe of life within each person who is united to Life himself. It is through that same vehicle of water that the Church, the body of Christ, is born, in which each member is called to participate in the work and ministry of the new Adam.

In speaking of the rational nature of the human person, St Basil the Great quotes Genesis 1.26, "And God said, let us make man (*anthrōpon*, Greek) in our image and likeness[3] and let them rule over the fish of the sea, the birds of the air, all the land creatures, and those that creep upon the earth."[4] St Basil says that the phrase "exerting dominion over the earth" means exercising reason, that characteristic of the human person that is the very image of God in man. He mourns the subjugation of human reason by the passions: "First the power to rule was conferred on you. O human, you are a ruling being. And why do you serve the passions as a slave? Why do you throw away your own dignity and become a slave to sin? For what reason do you make yourself a prisoner of the devil? You were appointed ruler of creation, and you have renounced the nobility of your own nature."[5] It is this self-absorption by the sinful passions that distorted the image of God in humanity and continues to distort it, turning the rational creature into the irrational, who then torments and further abuses that which is his or her vocation to rule in

[3] The words "in our image and likeness" are from the Septuagint.

[4] Author's translation.

[5] St Basil the Great, *On the Origin of Humanity, Discourse 1.8*, in *On the Human Condition*, trans. Sr Nonna Harrison, PPS 30 (Crestwood, NY: St Vladimir's Seminary Press, 2005), 37.

peace and love. St Basil goes on to make it quite clear that the vocation of humanity to rule the creation is shared equally by the sexes:

> But that nobody may ignorantly ascribe the name of human only to the man, it [the Scripture] adds, "Male and female he created them" [Gen 1.27]. The woman also possesses creation according to the image of God, as indeed does the man. The natures are alike of equal honor, the virtues are equal, the struggles are equal, the judgment alike. Let her not say, "I am weak." The weakness is in the flesh, in the soul is the power . . . through compassion it is vigorous in patient endurance and earnest in vigils. When has the nature of man been able to match the nature of woman in patiently passing through her own life? When has man been able to imitate the vigor of women in fastings, the love of toil in prayers, the abundance in tears, the readiness for good works?[6]

For humanity to truly rule over creation, it is thus essential to first rule over that inner cosmos, one's own soul, not only exercising reason in the image of God, but also approaching his likeness by acquisition of the virtues: "Therefore you have become like God through kindness, through endurance of evil, through communion, through love for one another and love for the brethren, being a hater of evil, dominating the passions of sin, that to you may belong the rule. . . . Rule the thoughts in yourself, that you may become ruler of all beings."[7] There is perhaps no better example of this *rule of all beings* than in the lives of the saints, who have exerted such intimate and powerful influence over the created order. From the time of the Roman persecutions of the Church, prime examples include Sts Euphemia (+September 16)[8] and Thekla (+September 24), both of whom at the time of their martyrdom were exposed to wild animals, which acted as though they were tame in the saints' presence.[9] More recent examples of saints popularly revered

---

[6]*On the Origin of Humanity, Discourse 1.18*, ibid., 45–46.

[7]*On the Origin of Humanity, Discourse 1.18, 19*, ibid., 46, 47.

[8]St Nikolai Velimirović, "Saint Euphemia," *The Prologue from Ochrid*, vol. 3, trans. Mother Maria (Birmingham, UK: Lazarica, 1986), 336.

[9]St Nikolai Velimirović, "Saint Thekla," in *Prologue from Ochrid*, 3:369.

in the West and East who also held converse with the beasts include, respectively, St Francis of Assisi (October 4)[10] and St Seraphim of Sarov (January 2).[11]

The rule of humanity is intended to extend beyond the animate to even the inanimate portion of creation. Christ invited the Apostle Peter, at his request, to join him as he walked upon the water (Mt 14.28–29). It was only when the apostle doubted—when he was cast about and distracted by fear and other passions—that he began to sink. The Fathers of the Church see Christ's walking on water as a powerful demonstration of his divinity and role as Creator. The Apostle Peter's deep love for Christ is manifested in his request to be commanded to come to the Lord on the water. Rather than asking to walk on the water, his ardent desire to be with Christ is demonstrated by the wording of his request. Ironically, Peter was noted to be "afraid of the lesser peril, the wind [rather than the sea]; such is the weakness of human nature."[12] The apostle's sinking, according to the Blessed Theophylact, was a result of "faintheartedness," for which he is rebuked by Christ. The commentator insists that the apostle did not doubt in everything:

> Inasmuch as he was afraid, he showed lack of faith; but by crying out, "Lord, save me," he was healed of his unbelief. This is why he hears the words "O thou of little faith" and not "O thou of no faith." Those in the boat were also delivered from fear, for "the wind ceased." And then, indeed, recognizing Jesus by these things, they confessed His divinity. For it is not an attribute of man to walk on the sea, but of God, as David says, "In the sea are Thy byways, and Thy paths in many waters." [Ps 76.19][13]

[10]For St Francis of Assisi, see, for example, "How St Francis Tamed the Very Fierce Wolf of Gubbio," in *The Little Flowers of St Francis*, trans. Raphael Brown (Garden City, NY: Image Books, 1958), 88–91.

[11]For a life of St Seraphim of Sarov, including his relationship with wild animals, see "Repose of the Venerable Seraphim the Wonderworker of Sarov," Orthodox Church in America, accessed September 17, 2015, *http://oca.org/saints/lives/2015/01/02/100008-repose-of-the-venerable-seraphim-the-wonderworker-of-sarov*.

[12]Blessed Theophylact, *Explanation of the Holy Gospel According to St Matthew*, 127.

[13]Ibid.

This encounter between the Apostle Peter and Christ on the water demonstrates an ongoing pattern in the relationship between Master and disciple:

> See also how Peter's later denial, return, and repentance were pre-figured by what happened to him here on the sea. Just as there he says boldly, "I will not deny Thee," so here he says, "Bid me to come on the water." And just as then he was permitted to deny, so now he was permitted to sink. Here the Lord gives His hand to him and does not let him drown, but there, by Peter's repentance, Christ drew him out of the abyss of denial.[14]

In the baptism of Christ in the Jordan, the entire material cosmos is touched by the holy, and thereby a uniquely paradoxical but deeply intimate communion is established between creation and Creator, in which all righteousness can be fulfilled. But humanity, as ruler of creation, must choose. Will the human person with all his or her frailties, like the Apostle Peter, strive to transcend his or her creation in the divine image in order to acquire the divine likeness? Reflecting on the command to "fill the earth" (Gen 1.28) given to the human rulers of creation by the Creator, St Basil provides an explanation for how the failed dominion of the first humans over creation might be reversed by a re-created humanity touched by the incarnate God through the waters of the Jordan River: "'Fill the earth.' Fill the flesh, which has been given you for service through good works. Let the eye be filled with seeing duties. Let the hand be filled with good works. May the feet stand ready to visit the sick, journeying to fitting things. Let every usage of our limbs be filled with actions according to the commandments. This is to 'fill the earth.'"[15]

The environment[16] is under significant strain and threat as humanity *multiplies and fills the earth* with its increasing numbers, industry,

[14]Ibid., 128.

[15]St Basil the Great, *On the Origin of Humanity, Discourse 2.5*, in *On the Human Condition*, 52.

[16]For an excellent discussion of the Eastern Church's understanding of the envi-

and the complexity of its many needs. The proper relationship between humanity as *ruler* and the creation it is *called* to rule provides the antecedent condition necessary for healing the cosmos. Instead of starting with a political process, humanity must address the problem, which is fundamentally spiritual in nature, at its root, spiritually. As St Basil has emphasized, "In truth, the human being is a small cosmos."[17] In the face of seemingly insoluble problems, we must first address the broken state of our own personal cosmos through repentance, actively striving to acquire the virtues so that we will become fit to rule creation and thereby aid in its healing. "You were born that you might see God, not that your life might be dragged down on the earth, not that you might have the pleasure of beasts, but that you might achieve heavenly citizenship."[18] This call *to see God*, which is no less than deification (*theōsis*, Greek), that is, to share by grace in the divine life as far as it is possible for creatures, changes the entire relationship not only between humanity and its Creator, but also between humanity and the creation we are called to rule. As rulers of creation we must lift up all of creation as an offering to its Creator. What kind of offering shall we make? We must strive with all our being to offer a creation that is both good and beautiful[19] back to its Creator. But we must ourselves be cleansed and healed before we can participate with Christ the high priest in making such an offering of thanksgiving and praise, a pure and holy Eucharist of the entire cosmos. The waters of the Jordan, transformed by Christ's baptismal touch, call out to all of creation to mystically unite with the members of his body and join in the re-creation and healing of the cosmos.

---

ronment, see A. G. Keselopoulos, *Man and the Environment: A Study of St Symeon the New Theologian*, trans. Elizabeth Theokritoff (Crestwood, NY: St Vladimir's Seminary Press, 2001).

[17] St Basil the Great, *On the Origin of Humanity, Discourse 2*, in *On the Human Condition*, 61.

[18] Ibid.

[19] The Greek word *kalos* embodies this double meaning of the inherent beauty of that which is morally good.

St Maximus the Confessor eloquently describes the process of deification (*theōsis*, Greek) that is intended for the entire creation, contrasting Christ's response to the Jewish authorities about his healing on the Sabbath, "My Father is still working, and so am I" (Jn 5.17), with the indication in the account of the creation that God "rested on the seventh day from all the works he had done" (Gen 2.2):

> God, as he alone knew how, completed the primary principles of creatures and the universal essences of beings once for all. Yet he is still at work, not only preserving these creatures in their very existence but effecting the formation, progress, and sustenance of the individual parts that are potential within them. Even now in his providence he is bringing about the assimilation of particulars to universals until he might unite creatures' own voluntary inclination to the more universal natural principle of rational being through the movement of these particular creatures toward wellbeing, and make them harmonious and self-moving in relation to one another and to the whole universe.... [O]ne and the same principle shall be observable throughout the universe, admitting of no differentiation by the individual modes according to which created beings are predicated, and displaying the grace of God to deify the universe. It is on the basis of this grace that the divine Logos, when he became man, said, *My Father is working even now, and I am working.* The Father approves this work, the Son properly carries it out, and the Holy Spirit essentially completes both the Father's approval of it all and the Son's execution of it, in order that the God in Trinity might be *through all and in all things* (Ephesians 4:6), contemplated as the whole reality proportionately in each individual creature as it is deemed worthy by grace, and in the universe altogether, just as the soul naturally indwells both the whole of the body and each individual part without diminishing itself.[20]

[20]St Maximus the Confessor, *Ad Thalassium 2: On the Preservation and Integration of the Universe*, in *On the Cosmic Mystery of Jesus Christ*, trans. Paul M. Blowers and Robert L. Wilken, PPS 25 (Crestwood, NY: St Vladimir's Seminary Press, 2003), 99–101.

Effectively, Christ's baptism in the Jordan River is the visible sign of the deifying grace of God as Holy Trinity acting through contact with water to unite the broken *particulars*, individual sinful human beings, into the wholeness and the *universality* of his body. By grace, as we attain to union with the divine life of the Holy Trinity, our vocation as deified rulers of creation will naturally follow.

> *When You, O Lord were baptized in the Jordan*
> *The worship of the Trinity was made manifest*
> *For the voice of the Father bore witness to You*
> *And called You His beloved Son.*
> *And the Spirit, in the form of a dove,*
> *Confirmed the truthfulness of His word.*
> *O Christ, our God, You have revealed Yourself*
> *And have enlightened the world, glory to You!*[21]

---

[21] Troparion in Tone 1 for the Feast of the Theophany of Our Lord and Savior Jesus Christ, Orthodox Church in America, https://oca.org/saints/troparia/2010/0 1/06/100106-feast-of-the-theophany-of-our-lord-and-savior-jesus-christ.

Plate 8

CHAPTER 7

Touching the Inner Cosmos

Before the Feast of Passover, Jesus, knowing that his hour had come when he would pass out of this world to the Father, and loving his own in the world, loved them to the end.[1] And during supper, when the devil had already placed in the heart of Judas Iscariot, the son of Simon, to betray him, and knowing that the Father had given all things into his hands and that he had come from God and was returning to God, he rose from the supper and removed his garments, and taking a towel, he tied it around himself. Then he poured water into a basin and began to wash the feet of the disciples and to wipe them with the towel with which he was encircled. Then he came to Simon Peter, who asked, "Lord, are you going to wash my feet?" Jesus answered and said to him, "What I am doing you do not understand now, but you will comprehend after these things." Peter said to him, "You may never wash my feet!" Jesus answered him, "If I don't wash you, you have no part with me." Then Simon Peter said to him, "Not my feet alone, but my hands and head as well!"

—John 13.1–9 (author's translation)

IN THIS GOSPEL PASSAGE, St John the Theologian, the beloved disciple, not only further illuminates but also deepens the mystery of the baptismal narrative presented in the Synoptic Gospels. It is no accident that Christ inaugurates his passion by returning to the metaphorical power of water, both as practical cleansing agent and

---

[1]The word end (*telos*) has a dual meaning, noted by the Church fathers in reference to this passage of Scripture. Not only does it have the meaning of "end in time," but also of "goal" or "purpose," "completion." A closely related Greek word, the adverb *teleiōs*, means "fully," "perfectly," or "completely." Thus the passage may also convey the sense that Christ loved them to perfection or completeness.

73

regenerative life-giving substance. The One who had already emptied himself by assuming human nature, who had no need of baptism but who nonetheless was baptized in the deepest humility to touch and heal his broken creation, now further reveals his true nature, his glory, to his disciples by this simple self-effacing act (see plate 8). In verse 1 it is noted that Christ, "loving his own in the world, he loved them *to the end.*" In their explanation of the kind and intensity of love the incarnate Word of God had for *his own in the world,* the Fathers of the Church emphasize the dual meaning of the Greek word *telos,* translated as "end" in this passage: "Seest thou how when about to leave them He showeth greater love? For the [phrase], 'having loved, He loved them unto the end,' showeth that He omitted nothing of the things which it was likely that one who earnestly loved would do."[2] The *end* was not only Christ's impending death and return to God, but also the occasion for demonstrating the *fullness* and *perfection* of his love for his own. In his passage from this world and return to God he does not leave behind the human nature he has assumed but deifies it. St Augustine goes further and identifies *telos* with Christ himself:

> For what mean these words, 'to the end,' but just to Christ? "For Christ is the end [*telos*] of the law," says the apostle, "for righteousness to everyone that believeth." [Rom 10:4] The end that consummates, not that consumes; the end whereto we attain, not wherein we perish. Exactly thus are we to understand the passage, "Christ our Passover is sacrificed" [1 Cor 5:7]. He is our end; into Him do we pass.[3]

It is through this action of washing, *touching* the most humble portion of his disciples' bodies with water, that Christ in the form of a slave demonstrates the nature of divinity as a foretaste of the cross. The incomprehensible is graphically demonstrated as the Lord of the universe humbles himself as a slave and shows his incredulous creatures the inverted nature of reality. The only way to deification, to *theōsis,* is through deep, ineffable humility, and that Way is Christ himself.

[2]St John Chrysostom, *Homilies on St John: Homily 70.1* (NPNF[1] 14:257).
[3]St Augustine, *Tractate 55.2 on the Gospel of John* (NPNF[1] 7:299).

In preparation for washing his disciples' feet, Christ deliberately strips down for this most menial of tasks like a common household slave. He chooses to personally wash their feet, the most defiled part of the body that is constantly in contact with the dust of the earth and thereby constantly in need of cleansing. His deliberate choice of performing this act during the supper also emphasizes that his purpose was not primarily practical—the disciples would have already been washed before the meal began. Rather, he intentionally touches the most defiled part of their bodies, using water as the means of contact. In further commenting on this passage, St Augustine emphasizes how the act of stripping his garments before washing his disciples' feet prefigures Christ's kenotic self-emptying at the crucifixion, that is, his willingness to suffer on behalf of his creatures, even his betrayer:

> When He emptied Himself in order to assume the form of a servant, He laid not down what He had, but *assumed that which He had not before*. When about to be crucified, He was indeed stripped of His garments, and when dead was wrapped in linen clothes: and all that suffering of His is our purification. When, therefore, about to suffer the last extremities [of humiliation,] He here illustrated beforehand its friendly compliances; not only to those for whom He was about to endure death, but to him also who had resolved on betraying Him to death. Because so great is the beneficence of human humility, that even the Divine Majesty was pleased to commend it by His own example; for proud man would have perished eternally, had he not been found by the *lowly God*.[4]

Christ reveals his divinity as the *lowly God* through this act of humble love. In anticipation of his coming passion, he further illuminates the purpose of his incarnation and the mystery of baptism for his disciples—not by words, but through action. Ironically, Judas apparently accepts Christ's humble gesture of love without protest, while Peter, from uncomprehending love, vociferously protests against this self-imposed indignity of his Master. St John Chrysostom identifies Peter's

[4]*Tractate* 55.7 (NPNF[1] 7:301, emphasis added).

response with the lack of any protests from the other disciples as an indication of his deep love for the Lord: "Someone might reasonably enquire, how none of the others forbade Him, but Peter only, which was a mark of no slight love and reverence. What then is the cause? He seemeth to me to have washed the traitor first, then to have come to Peter, and that the others were afterwards instructed from his case."[5] St John notes that when confronted with the impossibility of having any part in his Lord without being washed, he makes an equally vehement about-face, demanding that which he had so strongly rejected: "Vehement in deprecation, he becometh even more vehement in acquiescence; but both from love."[6]

This interaction between Christ and Peter illustrates the fundamental difference in the way in which Peter confronted his guilt in denying the Lord compared to how Judas acted following his betrayal of Christ. Like Judas, Peter was weak, sinful, and struggling with many passions, but the difference lay in his dread of being separated from Christ. He truly wanted to be fully immersed in Christ, to be washed clean. St Romanus the Melodist (sixth century) provides a powerful and deeply insightful poetic description of the contrast between the spiritual states of Judas and Peter in his *kontakion* called *On Judas*:

> When he plotted his trickery, when he planned your murder—the one who had been loved and rejected you, called and abandoned you, crowned and insulted you—then you, compassionate, long suffering, wanting to show the murderer your ineffable love for mankind, filled the basin, bowed your neck, became slave of slaves. And Judas presented you his feet for you to wash them. . . . Who ever saw one whose feet were being washed already hurrying to kick . . . ? The Lord washed and nourished. The traitor ran and gnashed his teeth like a wild untamed beast.[7]

---

[5] St John Chrysostom, *Homilies on St John: Homily* 70.2 (NPNF[1] 14:258).
[6] Ibid.
[7] St Romanus the Melodist, *On Judas*, in *On the Life of Christ: Kontakia*, 115–19.

But,

> Peter declined when the Only-Begotten inclined, eager to wash his
> feet, and he said, "Lord, Lord, you shall never wash my feet. . . . But,
> are you, the Potter of the world, also washing the feet of a vessel of
> clay . . . ?" When the apostle had used these words to the Teacher, he
> heard, "If I do not wash you now, I will not give you a part in me. . . ."
> When the Creator had spoken thus, fear and consternation fell on
> the disciple, and so he said, "My Lord, if you wash me, then not my
> feet only, but my whole body as well."
>
> The basin lay there already filled. The Savior stood there and
> the Redeemer had girded himself like a bought slave. . . . The fiery
> beings stopped in fear and the invisible choirs were stunned, as they
> saw the Incomprehensible voluntarily bending down and serving
> clay. . . . Peter stretches out his foot and the One who came from a
> virgin womb accepts it and washes it. And he does not only wash
> Peter, but Judas with him.[8]

Christ showed to his disciples that water applied and received in humility not only cleanses the one being washed, but also the one washing.

In the prologue to his first book on the Holy Spirit, St Ambrose
of Milan (fourth century) sees in Christ's washing of his disciples' feet
a cleansing extending beyond the physical. The humility Christ modeled in this action is at the heart of this interior washing. By providing
this example, he shows that the way to himself is through humility:
"Pour water into the basin, wash not only our feet but also the head,
and not only of the body, but also the footsteps of the soul. . . . Good is
the mystery of humility, because while washing the pollution of others
I wash away my own."[9] As in the sacrament of baptism, water in the
context of Christ's humility is more than mere metaphor. By following
the Master's example of humility in service to others, his servants experience interior cleansing. It is an image of the life in Christ following
baptism, of spiritual warfare: "Wash the steps of my mind that I may

[8]Ibid.
[9]St Ambrose, *On the Holy Spirit* 1, preface, §15 (NPNF[2] 10:95).

not sin again. Wash the heel of my soul, that I may be able to efface the curse, that I feel not the serpent's bite on the foot of my soul (see Gen 3.15), but as Thou Thyself hast bidden those who follow Thee, may tread on serpents and scorpions (see Lk 10.19) with uninjured foot."[10]

This image of interior cleansing through the water of humility is mirrored in the encounter between Christ and the fallen woman recorded in Luke's Gospel, in which she approaches Christ from behind as he is dining with the Pharisee and washes his feet with her tears and wipes them with her hair (Lk 7.36ff.). St Ambrose sees an icon of the Church and the relationship of its members to Christ in this encounter:

> The Church, then, both washes the feet of Christ and wipes them with her hair, and anoints them with oil, and pours ointment upon them, because not only does she care for the wounded and cherish the weary, but also sprinkles them with the sweet odor of grace.... Christ died once, and was buried once, and nevertheless He wills that ointment should daily be poured on His feet. What, then, are those feet of Christ on which we pour ointment? The feet of Christ are they of whom He Himself says: "What ye have done to one of the least of these ye have done to Me" [Mt 25.40]. These feet that woman in the Gospel refreshes, these feet she bedews with her tears; when sin is forgiven to the lowliest, guilt is washed away, and pardon granted. These feet he kisses, who loves even the lowest of the holy people ... in these the Lord Jesus Himself declares that He is honored.[11]

The unnamed woman of St Luke's Gospel, in all her brokenness and sorrow, already has learned the lesson Christ is teaching his disciples. Her humble repentance, driven by great love, has brought her to the feet of Christ. Like St Peter, she does not hold back. Her tears of repentance, flowing as living water (Jn 7.38), wash the feet of One who needs no cleansing but who nonetheless welcomes her with joy.

[10]Ibid.
[11]St Ambrose, Letter 41.22, 23 (NPNF² 10:449).

The spiritual Fathers of the Church have laid great emphasis on the cleansing power of tears, the living water bubbling up from within a person. St Maximus the Confessor linked humility, which Christ so vividly taught his disciples, directly with tears. "Humility consists in constant prayer combined with tears and suffering."[12] St Maximus' definition embraces both the humility of the incarnate Word of God on his way to his passion and the humility of a fallen but penitent creation, which is also bidden to take up its cross and follow after him. Whereas heartfelt tears of repentance and compunction over sin nourish the prayers of sinful human beings, Christ, who had no need of repentance, sheds tears of divine empathy for his fallen creatures and suffers with his creation, as only the God-Man is able in the fullness of a divinity defined by humility.

How, then, does one who has been wounded by sin begin to approach such humility? St Simeon the New Theologian emphasizes the great value of contemplating one's mortality, even the fear of eternal punishment, as an essential starting point for the spiritual life and as a foundation for humility:

He who does not attempt to evade the suffering engendered by the fear of eternal punishment, but accepts it wholeheartedly, and even adds to it as he can, will rapidly advance into the presence of the King of kings. And as soon as he has beheld the glory of God, however obscurely, his bonds will be loosed: fear, his tormentor, will leave him, and his heart's suffering will turn to joy. It will become a spring from which unceasing tears will flow visibly and which will fill him spiritually with peace, gentleness and inexpressible sweetness, as well as courage and the capacity to submit to God's commandments freely and unreservedly.[13]

Ultimately, humility must become action that touches others, and that action must flow from living tears of repentance. From that wellspring

[12] St Maximus the Confessor, *Four Hundred Texts on Love* 3.87, in *Philokalia* 2:97.

[13] St Simeon the New Theologian, *One Hundred and Fifty-Three Practical and Theological Texts* 67, in *Philokalia* 4:38.

can flow the exuberant, even extravagant, love of St Peter and the repentant woman, which will compel one to approach and touch Christ in the person of his poor and despised creatures.

Plate 9

CHAPTER 8

The Torture of God

The Saviour of us all, the Word of God, in His great love took to Himself a body and moved as Man among men, meeting their senses, so to speak, halfway. He became Himself an object for the senses, so that those who were seeking God in sensible things might apprehend the Father through the works which He, the Word of God, did in the body. . . . His body was for Him not a limitation, but an instrument, so that He was both in it and in all things, and outside all things, resting in the Father alone. At one and the same time—this is the wonder—as Man He was living a human life, and as Word He was sustaining the life of the universe, and as Son He was in constant union with the Father.

—St Athanasius, *On the Incarnation*[1]

THE INEFFABLE NATURE of the paradox embedded within this statement by St Athanasius, the great fourth-century father of the Church, is perhaps no more evident than when one contemplates the crucifixion of Christ (see plate 9). *His body was for Him not a limitation, but an instrument* . . . It was an instrument by which God could enter intimately, most profoundly, into the suffering of his creatures, even into their physical pain. St Athanasius' famous dictum that the Word of God "assumed humanity that we might become God,"[2] when understood in the context of the torture and crucifixion of the God-Man, should give every person who professes to be a Christian pause for reflection. The narrow and straight path toward *theosis*, of entering by grace into the divine life, is a journey marked in this life by a willingness to suffer in a manner similar to the Crucified One.

[1] St Athanasius, *On the Incarnation* §15, 17, PPS 3 (Crestwood, NY: St Vladimir's Seminary Press, 1993), 43–45.
[2] *On the Incarnation* §54, ibid., 93.

The various Gospel accounts of Christ's passion emphasize different aspects of his suffering and death. What is clearly evident from all of them is the intensely physical character of the torture that characterized this form of execution. Perhaps nowhere else in Christian doctrine is the absolute necessity of the physical humanity of Christ so apparent than in his passion, when he suffered in the flesh. Thus, sufficient details of his physical torment are presented in the Gospels to confirm his full participation in this most human of experiences, whether it was being spat upon, struck on the face and head, crowned with thorns, scourged, or pierced with nails.[3] The fullness of Christ's physical suffering is also echoed dramatically in the Liturgy of the Church during Holy Week:

> Every member of your Holy Body endured dishonor for us. Your Head, the thorns; Your Face, the spittings; Your Cheeks, the smitings; Your Mouth, the taste of vinegar mixed with gall; Your Ears, the impious blasphemies; Your Back, the lash; Your Hand, the reed; Your whole Body, stretched out on the Cross; Your Joints, the nails, and Your Side, the spear. O Almighty Savior, who in your mercy condescended to suffer for us, and set us free from suffering, having raised us up, have mercy on us.[4]

Scholars have noted in some detail the gruesome nature of the tortures endured by Christ in the Gospel reports,[5] which may not be fully appreciated by modern readers who, unlike the evangelists' contemporaries, may not be so familiar with the horrific character of this degrading form of execution. It is precisely through the sense of touch in its darker shades that such suffering could be inflicted and experienced.

Pain, or, more specifically, the ability to experience pain, is woven into the very fabric of biological existence. Among the panoply of

[3]See Mt 26.67–68; 27.29–30; Mk 14.65; 15.17–19; Lk 22.63–64; Jn 18.22; 19.1–3, 17–19; and 20.27.

[4]Holy Thursday Services, *Greek Orthodox Holy Week and Easter Services*, trans. Fr George L. Papadeas (South Daytona, FL: Patmos Press, 1996), 257.

[5]F. P. Retief and L. Cilliers, "Christ's Crucifixion as a Medico-Historical Event," *Acta Theologica*, supp. 7, 26.2 (2006): 294–309.

sensations that correspond to different aspects of touch, whether it be the gentle movement of air across the skin, a mother's loving caress, the comforting warmth of a fire on a winter's day, or the chill that drives one to seek out that consoling heat, touch as pain holds a unique place in human experience. Not only is the ability to sense pain essential for survival, but it can also represent the excess of sensation, at times even being a gross distortion or perversion of touch. A rare genetic disorder involving a familial kindred in Pakistan has highlighted this unique role of pain in protecting human beings from physical harm. Individuals born with the disorder are unable to experience physical pain.[6] A young boy with the condition who did not sense pain made his living as a street performer, inflicting increasingly harmful (and what would normally be quite painful) injuries to himself until he sustained fatal trauma after jumping off a roof to entertain his audience.[7] When other members of the kindred who also had the disorder were carefully assessed, they were able to accurately identify the sensations of touch, pressure, warmth, cold, proprioception (perceived orientation of a body part in space), and even tickle, but were unable to perceive pain. It was common for such individuals to have injured their tongues and lips early in life, and they not infrequently sustained fractures without fully appreciating the extent of their injuries.[8] More common examples of the dangers imposed by insensibility to pain are seen with peripheral neuropathies (nerve disorders) due to diabetes, AIDS, and leprosy (see chapter 5).

Clearly, the ability to perceive and appropriately avoid or withdraw from painful stimuli represents a critically important protective function for all organisms in a dangerous world. While this protective role of pain exerts itself throughout nature, human beings may be unique in their intentional exploitation of pain, not as a warning or protective mechanism, but purely for the purpose of causing distress and suffering

[6] J. J. Cox, et al., "An SCN9A Channelopathy Causes Congenital Inability to Experience Pain," *Nature* 444 (2006): 894–98.
[7] Ibid.
[8] Ibid.

in other creatures, especially others of their own species. Whether justi-
fied as necessary for the "greater good," an expression of the full fruition
of intense hatred, or even as a source of pleasure in sadomasochism, the
inflicting of pain as torture has transcended its physiological protective
function to become a form of pathologic discourse between human
persons. *Pathos*, the Greek word signifying "suffering," also refers to
the passions, those distortions of human qualities that were meant to
become virtues but instead have become reflections of fallen humanity's
spiritual illness. Anger, hate, lust, pride, and all the other passions are
not limited to the spiritual realm, but find a physical outlet for their full
expression in the material universe. The unique vulnerability of matter
as a body, as a sensate creature, is the capacity to experience physical pain and other forms of distress. As individual bodies interacting
with one another, human beings have the capacity and opportunity to
express those interactions through touch. The fundamental question
is: What form of touch? Will the passions or the virtues define the
touch exchanged between embodied human persons?

As was noted in chapter 1, a loss of normal contact between cells
in an organ can result in cellular "homelessness," or *anoikis*.[9] This condition of separation and isolation from other companion cells is not
consistent with survival and under normal circumstances leads to
programmed cell death, or *apoptosis*. However, as noted earlier, cancer
cells undergoing metastasis have lost their connectedness to their com-
panions and fail to respond to the signals for programmed cell death.
Exploiting their "homelessness," they embark on a journey of invasion
and destruction. A particularly disturbing characteristic of many metastatic cancer cells is their ability to produce pain by contact with cells
in the tissues they invade. A protein has recently been shown to be
heavily expressed on the surface of some types of invasive cancer cells
in proportion to the pain they produce where they have metastasized.[10]

[9]See S. M. Frisch and E. Ruoslahti, "Integrins and Anoikis," *Current Opinion in
Cell Biology* 9 (1997): 701–6.

[10]D. K. Lam et al., "TMPRSS2, a Novel Membrane-Anchored Mediator in Cancer Pain," *Pain* 156.5 (2015): 923–30.

Thus, even at a cellular level, pain as torture is inflicted by the invasive contact or touch of a cancer cell with its neighbors.

The incarnation made it possible for the Creator to intervene physically in the pathologic discourse of his impassioned creatures. God became Man so that he could even be tortured. Effectively, he, the Innocent One, took upon himself every torment his creatures' passions could offer. Physical contact between persons adds a "three-dimensional" character to each encounter, regardless of whether it is touch intended to bring comfort and healing or violent contact intended to cause pain and suffering. When more than one sense is engaged, the experience is more vivid, and the corresponding memories will be more deeply imbedded. One can state one's concern for another, even one's sincere good wishes for relief of the other's pain and suffering, but if what is stated verbally is accompanied by action, especially touch, a nonverbal expression of that same intent, then the words take on real substance. For example, it has been shown that at least some of the intense pain and distress inflicted by the surgeon's knife is mitigated by gentle massage administered in the hours and days after the initial wounding.[11] Although the traumatic nature of the encounter between surgeon and patient in the operating room is understood to be with the best of intentions, truly a compassionate healing act, reinforcing that intent by administering gentle massage during the postoperative recovery period restates that intention in a compelling nonverbal manner, where a sharp knife is replaced with soft hands. Just like communication through the spoken word, nonverbal communication through touch flows in two directions. The one touching intentionally is also touched; a connection has been made between two persons. The reciprocal nature of that contact may not be perceived consciously by the one who initiates the contact, especially in the context of a professional encounter between therapist and patient. And yet, the contact, through its reverberations within the person initiating it, can transcend professional boundaries,

[11] A. M. Mitchinson, H. M. Kim, J. M. Rosenberg, M. Geisser, M. Kirsh, D. Cikrit, and D. B. Hinshaw, "Acute Post-Operative Pain Management Using Massage as Adjuvant Therapy: A Randomized Trial," *Archives of Surgery* 142.12 (2007):1158–67.

opening one more fully to the suffering of the other. It is also not unreasonable to assume the same principle applies to the relationship formed between torturer and the victim of torture. Even though the intent of physical contact may be diametrically opposed to that of therapist and patient, nonetheless, the very intense nature of the encounter cannot help but have a reciprocal effect on the torturer. What if the recipient of the torture is divine; will that power of Divinity not be somehow felt within the innermost person of the torturer? Will the torturer be completely immune to the same power that brought healing to the woman with the flow of blood? Perhaps another aspect of these questions to contemplate is the proximity of torturer to victim. In St John's Gospel (19.1) it is simply stated that Pilate took Jesus and scourged (*mastigō*, Greek) him.[12] Clearly, in Pilate's position of authority, he delegated the actual torture, which he had instigated and for which he was ultimately responsible, to others, his soldiers. Nevertheless, even without laying a lash of the whip or causing a single tear in the flesh of Christ, he was in witnessing the outcome, *touching the suffering flesh of the Lord with his gaze,* entering to some intimate degree into that peculiarly horrible relationship between torturer and victim.

In the greatest of all ironies, Pilate then displays to the crowd the wounded, tortured Christ in the royal purple of his mockery, with the crown of thorns firmly planted on his head, and Pilate states, "Behold the man" (Jn 19.5).[13] The Church presents this and other details of the passion of the Lord on the evening of Holy Thursday, inviting each believer to look into the mirror presented by the many witnesses of

[12]See F. P. Retief and L. Cilliers, "Christ's Crucifixion as a Medico-Historical Event," for a detailed account of the specific form of scourging that preceded crucifixion. This was no mere whipping, but a flogging with instruments designed to tear the flesh, producing maximum pain and also intense blood loss, from which some victims died before being crucified.

[13]"*Idou ho anthrōpos*" spoken by Pilate refers to the tortured, humiliated Christ as the human being, not as the male of the species. Indeed, at that moment he is revealed in his abasement and intense suffering as the fullness of the image and likeness of God. See Fr John Behr, *Becoming Human* (Crestwood, NY: St Vladimir's Seminary Press, 2013), 26–39, for a beautiful discussion of Christ as the completion of God's project of creating a human being.

the tortured King of the Jews, not so much to condemn those who demanded his crucifixion, but that all may recognize their own vulnerability to the same passions that could motivate such acts. The extraordinary aspect of these events is the impact of increasingly close proximity to the Crucified One on those who tortured him and approved of the torture.

The selfsame centurion—in the Church's tradition later known as St Longinus, who, if not personally administering the physical punishment of Christ, at least oversaw the details—was the Roman officer who only a few hours later, upon witnessing Christ's death, could say, "Truly, this man was the son of God!" (Mk 15.39). The thieves crucified with Christ shared a common bond with him in their physical suffering. The great mystery is how the transforming power of proximity to the tortured God-Man made one thief more obdurate in his curses while at the same time, through the miracle of empathy, the eyes of the good thief were opened to behold the Paradise being crucified beside him.

There is another more elemental aspect of this mystery that should be considered. A perfect symmetry exists between the baptism of Christ in the Jordan River and his crucifixion. In the former, he sanctifies by his touch the very substance of biological life, and in the latter, by the voluntary extension of his body on the wood of the cross, he transforms an instrument of torture, degradation, and death into a source of healing unto eternal life. By his declaration to Nicodemus, Christ identifies his ultimate mission: "Just as Moses lifted up the serpent in the wilderness, so also the Son of Man must be lifted up, so that everyone who believes in him may have eternal life" (Jn 3.14–15).[14] The glory of God is hidden in paradox. Human beings may hate and revile him, rejecting every

[14] Author's translation. This image is often emphasized in the iconography of the crucifixion, in which Christ's body is extended in a serpentine manner on the cross (see plate 9). In this image of a serpent on a staff are reconciled the Jewish and Gentile nations, all of whom need healing. The brass serpent of Num 21.9 has its cognate in the serpent on the staff of the pagan healing deity, Aesculapius, who in his own way, by the grace of God, is a type of the Healer par excellence, Christ, *ho philanthrōpos*, the Lover of Mankind.

overture of Love himself and, when given the opportunity, will even torture and kill the God they can see and touch, and yet he transforms that worst form of human degradation into the greatest exaltation. The condescension of the Creator to become touchable is an act of humility beyond all human comprehension. In his foreknowledge, the Lord of Creation voluntarily accepts the full force of all the spiritual evil of the universe that is then transmuted into material expression and focused in the crucifixion. But when pure Love is wounded on the wood of the cross, the reciprocal nature of that contact rebounds through the wood upon the material as well as the spiritual order, leaving no aspect of reality untouched. After he is affixed to the cross, there is no place, no state of being, and no wrinkle in the fabric of space-time that is separated from his compassion. "Father, forgive them for they know not what they do" (Lk 23.34). The graves give up their dead, the veil of the temple is rent, and the earthquake gives utterance to the pain that will soon be tearing hell apart (Mt 27.51ff.). The tortured God cannot be dispensed with so easily. The deeper the suffering offered to the Creator by his creatures, the more intimate his embrace with his broken creation and the more fully he reveals himself in that suffering.

> Today is hung upon the Cross, He who suspended the earth amid the waters. A crown of thorns crowns Him, who is the King of Angels. He, who wrapped the heavens in clouds, is clothed with the purple of mockery. He, who freed Adam in the Jordan, received buffetings. He was transfixed with nails, who is the Bridegroom of the Church. He was pierced with a lance, who is the Son of the Virgin. We worship your Passion, O Christ. Show us also, your glorious Resurrection.[15]

---

[15]Fifteenth Antiphon from Holy Thursday Services, in *Greek Orthodox Holy Week and Easter Services*, trans. Fr George L. Papadeas (South Daytona, FL: Patmos Press, 1996), 238.

Plate 10

The Resurrection: Death Touched by Life

The sword of flame no longer guards the gate of Eden,
for a strange bond came upon it: the wood of the Cross.
The sting of Death and the victory of Hell were nailed to it.
But you appeared, my Saviour, crying to those in Hell:
"Be brought back
again to Paradise."

—St Romanus the Melodist[1]

HE TRADITIONAL ICON of the resurrection, which in reality depicts the events of Holy Saturday in the Orthodox tradition, is better known as the descent of Christ into hell (please see plate 10).[2] This event is not described directly in the Gospels, but is clearly alluded to both in the book of Acts and St Peter's First Epistle. In the former account, during St Peter's discourse before the Jewish leaders, he refers to Christ "whom God raised, loosing the labor pains of Death" (Acts 2.24).[3] In another reference to the events of Holy Saturday in his First Epistle, St Peter explicitly refers to Christ's being "put to death in the flesh but being made alive in the spirit, in which he went and preached to the *spirits in prison*" (1 Pet 3.18–19). St Matthew's account of the crucifixion,

[1]St Romanus the Melodist, *On the Victory of the Cross* 1, in *On the Life of Christ: Kontakia*, 155.

[2]For an excellent discussion of the history and theology underlying the iconographic depiction of the Resurrection, see L. Ouspensky and V. Lossky, *The Meaning of Icons*, trans. G. E. H. Palmer and E. Kadloubovsky (Crestwood, NY: St Vladimir's Seminary Press, 1999), 185–92.

[3]Author's translation. Death (*Thanatos*, Greek) is personified and given the ability to experience an extremely painful bellyache when it attempts to receive the incarnate God. Other early Christian authors exchange "*Thanatos*" with "*Hades*" (cf. St Polycarp of Smyrna), making an even stronger allusion to Death as a person.

which states that, following Christ's death, "the tombs were opened and many of the bodies of the saints who had fallen asleep were raised . . . and entered the holy city and were revealed to many" (Mt 27.52–53, author's translation), is also consistent with Christ's despoiling the realm of the dead. St John of Damascus (eighth century) interpreted St Paul's statement in the letter to the Philippians (2.10), "that every knee should bow to Him, of things in heaven, and things in earth and things under the earth," as a reference to Christ's descent into Hades.[4]

The image of a muscular Christ firmly grasping the hands of Adam and Eve as he drags them out of Hades is in stark contrast to the icon of the crucifixion in which the lifeless body of the same Lord is stretched upon the wood of the cross. It is precisely the paradox presented by the juxtaposition of these two icons wherein lies the central truth of the Christian faith. The mystery of the dead Christ forcefully overthrowing death and liberating those who had been captive to death can only be accessible through metaphor. A central feature of the metaphor is touch, but not an anemic, tentative touch. No, the metaphorical touch depicted in the icon of the descent into hell is the strong, confident grasp of the Rescuer who is pulling those trapped in their mortality out of death into Life. The profound irony within the paradox is that the very vulnerability, the apparent helplessness of the Crucified Victim has made it possible for divinity to directly confront mortality. The Word of God's union with our humanity in the incarnation made it possible for him to touch and thereby crush the ultimate end of our suffering, death.

St John of Damascus sheds additional light on the paradox by emphasizing the unique character of the relationship between the divinity and humanity of the God-Man: "We say that God suffered in the flesh, but never that His divinity suffered in the flesh, or that God suffered through the flesh."[5] He insists that the divinity of the Word of God remained inseparable from the soul and body even at the Lord's death, so that at the same time in his humanity he lay as a

---

[4]St John of Damascus, *An Exposition of the Orthodox Faith* 3.29 (NPNF[2] 9:72–73).

[5]Ibid., 3.26 (NPNF[2] 9:71).

lifeless corpse in the tomb, in his divinity he was never separated from the Father and the Holy Spirit. It is through the portal of his assumed human mortality that the life-giving Creator voluntarily gains direct access to and tramples upon death. The Damascene goes on to reason that "since our Lord Jesus Christ was without sin (*for He committed no sin, He Who took away the sin of the world, nor was there any deceit found in His mouth* [Is 53.9]) He was not subject to death, since death came into the world through sin [Rom 5.12]."[6] Even the icon of the Feast of the Nativity, in which the Church celebrates the Word made flesh, anticipates the icon of the descent into hell, emphasizing the primary mission of the God-Man. The manger has the distinct appearance of a sarcophagus, the swaddling clothes are his winding sheet, and the cave in which the Savior is born prefigures the grave in which he will destroy death. Each of these mundane material realities acquires deeper profound meanings through the metaphor buried within touch. When the divine Child touches the ordinary, it becomes extraordinary; where there was a poverty of meaning, now the fullness of the meaning hidden therein is illuminated by his touch.

It is with this metaphorical understanding of touch that one can then approach the triumphant encounter between God at the very moment of his greatest abasement as a lifeless corpse with death and the devil. Borrowing imagery from St Gregory of Nyssa,[7] the Damascene identifies the encounter almost in a wry sense, as the most profound and amazing of holy deceptions!

> Wherefore death approaches, and swallowing up the body as a bait is transfixed on the hook of divinity, and after tasting of a sinless and life-giving body, perishes, and brings up again all whom of old he swallowed up. For just as darkness disappears on the introduction

[6]Ibid., 3.27 (NPNF[2] 9:72).

[7]". . . the Deity was hidden under the veil of our nature, that so, as with ravenous fish, the hook of the Deity might be gulped down along with the bait of flesh, and thus, life being introduced into the house of death, and light shining in darkness, that which is diametrically opposed to light and life might vanish; for it is not in the nature of darkness to remain when light is present, or of death to exist when life is active." St. Gregory of Nyssa, *The Great Catechism* 24 (NPNF[2] 5:494).

of light, so is death repulsed before the assault of life, and brings life to all, but death to the destroyer.[8]

Thus is the effect of the medicine of immortality[9] upon contact with death. The icon of the descent into hell is then most profoundly an image of the Eucharist, of communion, par excellence; but death cannot commune with Life and survive the experience.

St John of Damascus explains how the hypostatic union of the two natures in Christ makes possible the paradox of a vibrant, powerful King of Glory who can despoil hell while at the same time he rests in the grave:

> For body and soul received simultaneously in the beginning their being in the subsistence of the Word, and although they were severed from one another by death, yet they continued, each of them, having the one subsistence of the Word. . . . For at no time had either soul or body a separate subsistence of their own, different from that of the Word, and the subsistence of the Word is for ever one, and at no time two. So that the subsistence of Christ is always one. For, although the soul was separated from the body topically, yet hypostatically they were united through the Word.[10]

Visually, the icon of the descent into hell presents the destruction of death and hell as an accomplished fact—Christ has trampled down death by his death. The intense immediacy of this universal moment in cosmic time reverberates into the past, present, and future. Thus, wherever and whenever the Holy Offering is made, the full reality of Golgotha and the empty tomb is present. Christ dies, descends into hell, and arises in triumph at every celebration of the Eucharist. Pascal's statement that "Jesus will be in agony even to the end of the world"[11] resonates with the continuing temporal aspect of the truth revealed through the icon.

---

[8]St John of Damascus, *An Exposition of the Orthodox Faith*, 3.27 (NPNF² 9:72).
[9]St Ignatius of Antioch, *Letter to the Ephesians* 20.2.
[10]St John of Damascus, *Exposition of the Orthodox Faith* 3.27 (NPNF² 9:72).
[11]Blaise Pascal, *Pascal's Pensées*, trans. W. F. Trotter (New York: E. P. Dutton, 1958), 148.

The universal nature of the event depicted in the icon should not overshadow what is also a profoundly personal and deeply intimate encounter with every human soul that is at the heart of the descent into hell. Just as with the Greek *imperfect* tense, there is a continuing process that was initiated on Holy Saturday, which directly affects the life of every person to whom Christ announces his triumph over death through this icon. Death as metaphor merges with the raw reality of individual human mortality. In the icon, Christ not only despoils Hades of his dead, but, with the assent of each soul held captive to death, he restores the conditions for Eden. The descent into Hades is an image of *theōsis*. Through his embrace of suffering and death in his humanity, the God-Man makes bold to enter and touch the darkest recesses of our being to show us the way back to Life. The descent into hell becomes the ultimate healing encounter between the soul saturated with death and the Crucified One, whom death cannot absorb. The life lived within the sacraments of the Church, his body, is a continual, ever-deepening journey into the mystery of his union with death. Unlike Hades, can we not rejoice in the labor pains of our own suffering unto life as he cleanses, purifies, and washes away the stains of our passions?

> Today, hell cries out groaning:
> My dominion has been shattered.
> I received a dead man as one of the dead,
> But against Him I could not prevail.
> From eternity I had ruled the dead,
> But behold, He raises all.
> Because of Him do I perish.
> Glory to thy cross and resurrection, O Lord.[12]

[12]From the *Vespers and Divine Liturgy of St Basil the Great for Great and Holy Saturday*, Fr Paul Lazor, ed. (Latham, NY: Department of Religious Education, Orthodox Church in America, 1986), 16.

Plate 11

CHAPTER 10

Taste and See: Faith, Touch, and Metaphor

O taste and see that the Lord is good.

—Ps 33.8 (LXX)

All the angels in heaven marvel at things of earth;
that humans born of earth, who inhabit what is below,
are lifted up in thought and attain what is on high
as partakers in Christ crucified.
For together they all eat his Body.
As they fervently approach the Bread of Life,
from it they hope for immortal salvation.
Though to the senses it appears as bread,
spiritually it makes them holy, for it is
the heavenly bread of incorruption.

—St Romanus the Melodist[1]

O F THE MANY DISTRESSING CHANGES that occur as a loved one gradually succumbs to the ravages of an advanced cancer or other terminal illness, the progressive loss of appetite and diminished oral intake that results is in many ways the most difficult symptom to witness. Nourishment represents more than just satisfying a biological necessity; it is the very essence of participation in life and in the community of the living. Death is often perceived as a breaking of this communion with the living; thus, dying persons feel their increasing isolation intensely. To no avail, concerned family members will urge the dying person to eat, not only to somehow restore the health that cannot be regained, but also to reverse the growing separation and bridge

---

[1]St Romanus the Melodist, *On the Five Loaves* 1, in *On the Life of Christ: Kontakia*, 89.

the gulf between life and death. At no other moment in one's existence is this sharp contrast between the ordinary, comforting routine of everyday life and the harsh finality of human mortality so evident than when being confronted by the imminent demise of a loved one, except perhaps when denial fails in the confrontation with one's own mortal condition.

Before Christ raises Lazarus, he allows his friend's sisters, Martha and Mary, to separately express their very human regret: "Lord, if you had been here, my brother would not have died" (Jn 11.21, 32). This same desperate searching for solutions—whether in urging the dying person to eat, begging physicians for futile nutritional interventions, or even continued rumination on possible rescue strategies after the death—remains as part of the human response to the horrible impotence of the mortal condition. Christ, who will momentarily demonstrate by raising Lazarus that he is indeed the resurrection and the life, does not minimize the horrible tragedy of human mortality as embodied in the plight of his friend, but sanctifies human grief with his tears (Jn 11.25, 35). He in no way shuns viewing death in all its terrible reality: he even allows his friend to undergo corruption before raising him so that his disciples will understand that he has come into the world precisely for the purpose of confronting death in all its ugliness and, through his death, of liberating humans held captive to sin by their mortality.

For the two disciples grieving the loss of their rabbi as they made their way to Emmaus, it was profoundly significant that they did not recognize and know the risen Lord until he blessed and broke the bread and gave it to them (Lk 24.30). It was only in the breaking of the bread that they began to understand that in his suffering, the Crucified One had entered his glory (see plate 11). Thus, real nourishment in the forms of the sanctified bread and wine, sustenance transcending and transforming death, must be distributed to each person seeking intimate communion with the divine. This medicine of immortality[2] is the nourishment unto real life that unconsciously is at heart of the

[2]St Ignatius of Antioch, *Letter to the Ephesians* 20.2.

desperate search of loved ones who seek to rescue the dying from the isolation and separation of their mortality.

It is no accident that the material means by which the believer may seek an ever-deeper and more intimate embrace with God is something so basic as bread and wine. Considering that the search for nourishment as the most essential requirement for sustaining life has been the primary occupation of human beings throughout much of human history, it only seems natural that our pathway to the divine in this material existence, where hunger and thirst are dominant motivations, would involve material that can be ingested. St Basil the Great, in his contemplation of the creation, emphasized the inherent interconnectedness of the entire cosmos. While he describes the many and varied connections between different aspects of the created order, from the most basic elements combined in different ways to form ever-more-complex structures and functions, he also emphasizes the transcendent beauty of the simple: "A single plant, a blade of grass is sufficient to occupy all your intelligence in the contemplation of the skill which produced it."[3] Thus, a continual ascending process of exchanges in nature has been initiated by the Creator—water and the basic elements sustaining life with the warmth of the sun—eventually leading to the formation of grapes and wheat.

And yet in another exchange, as in the feeding of the five thousand, Christ shows the essential necessity of the creature to *cooperate* with the Creator: "You give them something to eat" (e.g., Mk 6.37). The creature must participate in the creative acts of God by *touching and processing* these materials before offering these gifts back in the transformed states of bread and wine to God, saying "Amen" by his or her actions directed to the One who will ultimately give himself back to his creatures through those same elements. When the bread and wine are brought to the Eucharist, the faithful, as the body of Christ, join the Virgin in saying, "Let it be to me according to your word" (Lk 1.38). It is a cascade of metaphors, drawn from the most basic of human experiences, leading to the ultimate Truth behind all metaphor. The simpler

[3]St Basil the Great, *The Hexaemeron* 5.3 (NPNF[2] 8:77).

and more fundamental the metaphors, the more tangible, the better they speak to the universal human condition, and the more effective they will be in bringing healing to it.

Unfortunately, the Western mind is tormented by the desire to know mechanism rather than simply being still in the presence of ineffable mystery. St Ephrem the Syrian highlights the mystery inherent in the transformative acts of God in his discussion of the miracle of the feeding of the five thousand, which is a type of the greater miracle occurring in the eucharistic mystery: "That which [people] effect and transform in ten months with toil, his ten fingers effected in an instant. For he placed his hands beneath the bread as though it were earth, and spoke over it as though thunder. The murmur of his lips sprinkled over it like rain, and the breath of his mouth [was there] in place of the sun."[4] The truly remarkable thing is that God, in his infinite compassion for his creatures, desires our active participation in the mystery to the degree we are able. He bids us modify that which he created ex nihilo through our own modest efforts into the basic elements of food and drink that he will then transform into his very Presence, if we would but believe and trust him at his word. St Basil the Great, a preeminent scholar and intellectual of his time, addresses the speculative curiosity of the human being in attempting to understand the *how* of God's creative acts: "If there is anything in this system which might appear probable to you, keep your admiration for the source of such perfect order, for the wisdom of God. Grand phenomena do not strike us the less when we have discovered something of their wonderful mechanism.... At all events let us prefer the simplicity of faith to the demonstrations of reason."[5] The Orthodox Christian prayers said before communion fully embrace the power of metaphor, even fairly earthy metaphors, when confronted by the mystery of the divine condescension in the eucharistic meal. St John Chrysostom reminds us in very direct terms who we are in relation to the Person present in the Eucharist:

[4]St Ephrem the Syrian, *Commentary on Tatian's Diatessaron*, in ACCS:NT 2:91.
[5]St Basil the Great, *Hexaemeron* 1.10 (NPNF² 8:57).

And as you willed in the cave to lie in a manger of dumb animals, take it upon yourself now to enter the manger of my dumb soul and into my soiled body. And as you did not refuse to enter and eat with sinners in the house of Simon the leper, so also deign to enter into the house of my soul, leper and sinner that I am. And as you did not cast out the harlot, a sinner like me, who came and touched you, so have compassion on me the sinner who now comes to touch you. And as you did not abhor the kiss of her sinful and unclean mouth, do not abhor my mouth, more stained and unclean than hers, nor my sordid and unclean and shameless lips, nor my more unclean tongue. But let the fiery coal of your most pure body and of your most precious blood bring sanctification, illumination, and strengthening of my lowly soul and body.[6]

The metaphors in the prayers before communion emphasize the condescension and infinite compassion of God while reminding us of the one essential condition for our participation in the encounter with the divine: humility.

The transformative power of the eucharistic metaphor within the Church is most manifest in the lives of her saints. As St Ignatius of Antioch makes his way to his martyrdom in Rome in the early second century of the Christian era, he begs his fellow Christians to not intervene and prevent this ultimate form of communion with his crucified Lord, "whose life, if we do not choose willingly to die for truth in likeness of his passion, is not in us."[7] At every Divine Liturgy, during which the Eucharist is celebrated, the believer encounters the crucified and risen Lord. The continued ascent and sharing in the divine life through regular communion can only draw Christians more deeply into the mystery of the love, which is manifested as Christ crucified and resurrected. So, St Ignatius pleads with the faithful to let him draw ever

---

[6]"Daily Prayers for Orthodox Christians," in *The Synekdemos*, ed. N. M. Vaporis (Brookline, MA: Holy Cross Orthodox Press, 1986), 84.

[7]St Ignatius of Antioch, *Letter to the Magnesians* 5.2, in *Ignatius of Antioch: The Letters*, trans. Alastair Stewart, PPS 49 (Yonkers, NY: St Vladimir's Seminary Press, 2013), 47.

nearer to that mystery where the reality of Christian martyrdom and eucharistic metaphor merge: "I know what is right for me. Now I am beginning to be a disciple."[8] And:

> Leave me to be bread for the beasts, through which I may be able to attain to God. I am God's wheat and through the beasts' teeth I shall be found to be pure bread for Christal....I am not directing you like Peter and Paul. They were apostles, I am a condemned criminal. They were free, I am still a slave. But if I should suffer I shall become a freedman of Jesus Christ, and I shall rise up free in him.[9]

The dilemma that each person faces when confronted with the death of a loved one or his or her own mortality is resolved within the eucharistic paradox. The very phenomenon that threatens dissolution and separation has now become the means of eternal union, of completion, an integrity transcending every threat. The mystery of the action of the dead Christ entering the realm of death on Holy Saturday is recapitulated every time he enters the dark places of our being through communion. Just as death could not commune with the source of Life, so also may our dead souls be revived unto eternal life, if we, with the Virgin, can only say, "Yes, let it be to me according to your word" (Lk 1.38).

---

[8] St Ignatius of Antioch, *Letter to the Romans* 5.3, in *The Letters*, 71.
[9] Ibid. 4.1, 3, ibid., 69, 71.

Plate 12

CHAPTER 11

The Touch of Doubt

With his meddling right hand, Thomas explored
your life-giving side, Christ God;
for the doors being shut
when you entered,
he cried out with the rest of the apostles,
"You are our Lord and our God."

—St Romanus the Melodist[1]

Thomas, one of the Twelve, who was called the Twin, was not with
them when Jesus came. The other disciples said to him, "We have seen
the Lord." But he replied, "Unless I see in his hands the mark of the
nails and I place my hand in his side, I will not believe." And after eight
days his disciples were again inside, and Thomas was with them. The
doors having been locked, Jesus came and stood in their midst and said,
"Peace be with you." Then he said to Thomas, "Bring your finger here
and behold my hands, and bring your hand and place it in my side, and
no longer be unbelieving, but believe." Thomas replied and said to him,
"My Lord and my God!" Jesus said to him, "Because you have seen me,
you have believed? Blessed are those who not seeing yet believe."

—John 20.24–29 (author's translation)

THIS EXCHANGE PRESENTS the very evidence that a true empiri-
cist like Thomas would demand and that Christ, in his love and
condescension to human need, offers freely (see plate 12). But perhaps
the most significant part of the encounter is what Thomas and the
other disciples hear after he has touched the wounds of the risen Lord

[1]St Romanus the Melodist, *On the Apostle Thomas,* Prelude 1, in *On the Life of*
Christ: Kontakia, 183.

and made his profound statement of faith. Is not Christ's response to Thomas an allusion to the experience of the two disciples who recognized him in the breaking of the bread? "Blessed are those who, not seeing, yet believe."

The Fathers of the Church emphasize the importance of the doubting disciple's absence at the time of the initial appearance of the risen Lord to the other disciples: "It was not an accident that that particular disciple was not present. The divine mercy ordained that a doubting disciple should, by feeling in his Master the wounds of the flesh, heal in us the wounds of unbelief. The unbelief of Thomas is more profitable to our faith than the belief of the other disciples. For the touch by which he is brought to believe confirms our minds in belief, beyond all question."[2] Another ancient commentator, Peter Chrysologus, raises some disturbing questions about the possible motivations driving the doubting disciple's bold demand for direct evidence, a demand that may resonate very well with the modern insistence on absolute, empirical evidence:

> Why does the hand of a faithful disciple in this fashion retrace those wounds that an unholy hand inflicted? . . . Why does the harsh curiosity of a servant repeat the tortures imposed by the rage of persecutors? Why is a disciple so inquisitive about proving from his torments that he is the Lord, for his pains that he is God, and from his wounds that he is the heavenly Physician? . . . Why Thomas, do you alone, a little too clever a sleuth for your own good, insist that only the wounds be brought forward in testimony to faith? What if these wounds had been made to disappear with the other things? What a peril to your faith would that curiosity have produced? Do you think that no signs of his devotion and no evidence of the Lord's resurrection could be found unless you probed with your hands his inner organs that had been laid bare with such cruelty?[3]

---

[2]Pope St Gregory the Great, *Gospel Homilies* 26, in ACCS:NT 4b:367.
[3]Peter Chrysologus, Sermon 84.8, ibid.

But the commentator answers his many rhetorical questions by affirming the necessity of the kind of evidence that St Thomas demanded and defending the motives of the disciple: "Brothers, his devotion sought these things, his dedication demanded them so that in the future not even godlessness itself would doubt that the Lord had risen. But Thomas was curing not only the uncertainty of his own heart but also that of all human beings. . . . For the only reason the Lord had kept his wounds was to provide evidence of his resurrection."[4]

Contemporary thought takes great comfort and pride in the scientific basis for the assumptions of daily existence. Perhaps only a few fully appreciate that the scientific method is grounded on profound skepticism and depends on narrowly defined hypotheses (suppositions about specific questions or problems), which can be tested through careful observation. It is only when the reproducible outcomes of repeated observations contradict the likelihood that such outcomes are merely the product of chance that a particular hypothesis begins to acquire some level of authority. It is always understood that additional evidence may yet disprove the hypothesis and thus dethrone a highly respected hypothesis that may have acquired the dignity of being called a theory. Unfortunately, this healthy skepticism is often forgotten when scientific theories acquire, over time, a dignity not unlike religious dogma. Whether we are aware or not, most of us as members of the human race, of necessity, rely heavily on an understanding of the natural world formed from scientists' careful consideration of the available empirical evidence—the greater reproducibility of a given observation, the more reliable the assumptions made. However, the absolute necessity imposed by the method to reduce a given question to a narrowly defined, testable hypothesis must be tempered with a humble recognition that one's own biases, or else limited understanding, may preclude asking the right questions and could impair the interpretation of the experimental results. Nevertheless, the scientific method is an incredibly powerful tool for asking specific, well-defined questions that in aggregate can provide profound and beneficial insights; witness the

[4]Ibid., 367–68.

growth of scientific medicine with the advent of the germ theory in the nineteenth century and the subsequent iterations to the present-day revolution in cellular and molecular biology. However, when questions that are not amenable to such a reductionist, hypothesis-driven approach arise, such as basic existential questions or questions about the nature of the person, the scientific method is out of its element. It can only address very specific—albeit fascinating—questions about the needles on the forest floor and occasionally hint at the presence of the trees, and yet it never comes close to grasping the essence of the entire forest. Herein lies the problem of faith versus science. They are different modes of understanding that need not be in conflict, because they are circumscribed by different assumptions.

Is faith merely a sense of trust in the reproducibility of expected outcomes? In this sense, one could express deep faith that the earth will continue to rotate around the sun and produce predictable transitions between day and night. But what of phenomena that are beyond any conception of the ordinary, that defy common sense or the safety of reproducible empiric observation? This seems to be the difficult terrain that St Thomas was attempting to traverse after hearing of the Lord's resurrection from the dead. Beginning with the questioning empiricism and doubts of the scientist, he arrived at a very different ultimate destination than what would be expected as a result of pure empirical observation alone.

St John Chrysostom highlights the significance of the delay of eight days between Christ's first postresurrection appearance (with Thomas absent) and the second one, in which the doubting disciple *was* present:

> And why doth He not appear to him straightway, instead of "after eight days"? In order that being in the mean time continually instructed by the disciples, and hearing the same thing, he might be inflamed to more eager desire, and be more ready to believe for the future. But whence knew he that His side had been opened? From having heard it from the disciples. How then did he believe

partly, and partly not believe? Because this thing was very strange and wonderful. But observe, I pray you, the truthfulness of the disciples, how they hide no faults, either their own or others', but record them with great veracity.[5]

Thomas, by God's mercy, is given the time he needs to be prepared for his direct encounter with the Truth. It is in the community of the faithful that his initial incredulity in the face of the seemingly impossible is addressed so that the doubting disciple, in his first faltering steps toward faith, is doubting his own doubts by the time he meets the risen Lord. The extraordinary thing is that by the divine condescension in fulfilling Thomas's need for direct tangible evidence, the once-doubting disciple is transformed through the sense of touch into the most faithful champion of the two natures of Christ!

> But as soon as Thomas touched the Lord's side, he was revealed as a superb theologian, proclaiming the two natures and single hypostasis of the one Christ. Thomas refers to the human nature of Christ, calling Him *Lord*; for the term, "Lord" [(Κύριος] is applied not just to God, but to men as well. (Thinking that Jesus was the gardener, Mary Magdalene had said to Him, *Sir* [(Κύριε], *if thou have borne Him hence . . .*). But when Thomas cries out, *My Lord and My God*, he confesses Christ's divine essence and affirms that the names *Lord* and *God* refer to one and the same Person.[6]

The person of Thomas struggling with his doubts embodies all the natural curiosity, inquisitiveness, and questioning nature of the human race. He is the protoscientist driven to seek empirical evidence of the reality of a phenomenon that is ultimately beyond human comprehension. From a purely "scientific" perspective, Thomas's physical encounter with Christ's wounds provides compelling evidence that the living Person standing before him has also sustained the wounds of crucifixion. Following the dispassionate scientific approach, he should then

[5]St John Chrysostom, *Homily 87.1 on the Gospel According to St John* (NPNF[1] 14:327).

[6]Blessed Theophylact, *Explanation of the Holy Gospel According to John*, 301.

affirm the evidence as he has experienced it: a victim of crucifixion stands before him alive and well. But he doesn't stop here. He declares unequivocally his faith that transcends the physical evidence by stating, "My Lord and my God!" Here is where science and the constant demand for more evidence are confronted by faith. Christ, in his love for Thomas and all those who, like Thomas, struggle with doubt, condescends to directly encounter his hesitation and doubt. By so doing, he has made it possible for those who, unlike Thomas, will believe without touching his wounds. The Blessed Theophylact (eleventh century) further clarifies:

> By declaring blessed those who have not seen, and yet have believed, the Lord teaches us that faith means the acceptance of things not seen. He is referring first to the disciples who believed without touching His side or the print of the nails, and second to those who would later believe [without any physical confirmation]. . . . The question arises: how can an incorruptible body display the mark of nails and be touched by human hands? The answer is that such things are possible as part of the divine *economia*: they are manifestations of God's condescension and love for man. By entering the room *when the doors were shut*, Christ makes it absolutely clear that after the resurrection His body is altered: it is now light and subtle, free of all material coarseness. But to confirm that it is indeed their Lord and Master Who has appeared to them, He permits his resurrected body, bearing the wounds of the crucifixion, to be touched. . . . Do you see . . . how, in order to save one doubting soul, the Lord did not spare His own dignity but condescended to bare his side? Neither should we despise even the least of our brethren.[7]

Paradoxically, through one disciple's doubt and weakness, the enduring faith of future disciples is assured. St Romanus, the Melodist (sixth century) elaborates upon this theme in his *kontakion* about St Thomas.

[7]Ibid., 301–2.

For the definition of this faith was signed surely for me through Thomas's hand. By touching Christ it became like the pen of a swiftly writing scribe, writing for believers the place from where faith springs up. From there, the thief drank and came to his senses again. From there, disciples watered their hearts. From there, Thomas drew the knowledge of the things he sought. First he drinks, then gives to drink, having momentarily doubted, he persuaded many to say, "*You are our Lord and our God.*"[8]

The physical evidence that Thomas is invited to inspect is only a beginning, but, in human terms, perhaps an essential beginning for many on the road to faith. St John the Theologian begins his first epistle by restating this evidence and its ultimate purpose: "That which was from the beginning, which we heard, which we saw with our eyes, which we observed, and which *our hands touched*, concerning the Word of Life . . . what we saw and heard we announced to you so that you might have fellowship with us as we have fellowship with the Father and his Son, Jesus Christ" (1 Jn 1.1–3, author's translation). The faith of Thomas was not born from a purely objective examination of empirical evidence. It could only emerge from the interface between a conscious acknowledgment of the evidence and an interaction between persons made initially possible through the senses. For the faith spoken so eloquently in Thomas's declaration to Christ is not the affirmation of an idea or a fact, but a commitment of absolute trust in a Person. It is the necessary element, the sine qua non, for the journey toward union with the unknowable God, who yet through a relationship with his incarnate Word can be known. Not by the rules of hypothesis-driven investigation by a dispassionate observer, but only by complete immersion in a relationship with the Other, can this Truth be known. There remains one point of common ground, however, between the empirical approach of the scientist in search of knowledge and the journey toward *theōsis*. To get started, both the scientist and the believer must

---

[8]St Romanus the Melodist, *On the Apostle Thomas*, in *On the Life of Christ: Kontakia*, 184 (emphasis added).

risk doing the experiment. We cannot bury the talent given to us, nor can we ignore the evidence, but we need to understand that the evidence being presented to us may not be in the form of our choosing.

In all humility, let us fully trust the One who said, "This is my Body and this is my Blood" (cf. Mt 26.26–28) to feed us with himself, not being further concerned with mechanism, but only with loving obedience to his command. And then, perhaps we will begin to experience the truly reproducible outcome of the *experiment* of faith: "Taste and see, that the Lord is good" (Ps 33.8). The relationship broken through ingestion of that which was forbidden is now healed through obedient consumption of the fruit of the tree of life. Paradise has stooped down to earth, so that we might pluck its fruit and live.

> Most High, by grace strengthen me in soul and flesh, and save me
> so that I may touch your side. Receiving your grace,
> your Blood and your Body, I am delivered from my evils,
> so that I may find forgiveness of transgressions.
> Thomas, by handling, has now come to know your glory,
> but I am frightened, for I know your counsels,
> I know my works. Conscience troubles me.
> Spare me, my Saviour, spare me, Compassionate,
> that by works and words I may unceasingly cry to you,
> *"You are our Lord and our God."*[9]

---

[9] Ibid., 190–91.

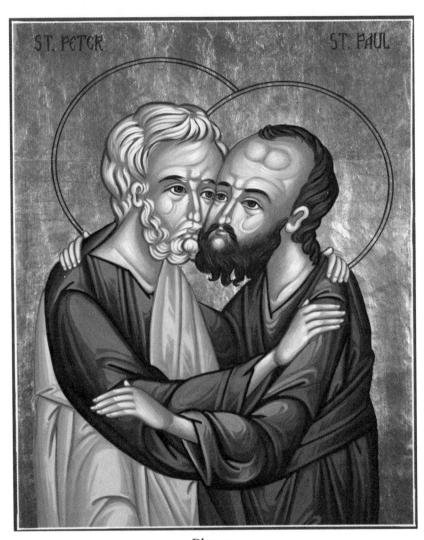

Plate 13

CHAPTER 12

The Kiss of Peace: Touch and Reconciliation

*Our whole life, lived in love to our neighbour and nature, is nothing
more than one long kiss.*

—Kristoffer Nyrop[1]

C ONFLICT IS SUCH A COMMON aspect of human experience that
one might be tempted to think it the norm. And yet, the Word
became flesh to free us from the mortal wounds, the passions, that
are at the heart of human conflict. Perhaps one of the most profound
examples of this transformation effected by the power of the Holy
Spirit within the early life of the Church was the resolution of a public
quarrel between Sts Paul and Peter. The Apostle Paul gives his perspective of the situation in his Letter to the Galatians: "When Cephas
came to Antioch, I withstood him to his face, because he stood con-
demned. For before certain persons who came from James he ate with
the Gentiles; but after they came, he drew back and separated himself,
fearing those of the circumcision" (Gal 2.11–12, author's translation).
The Fathers of the Church offer various explanations for this apparent
conflict between the two apostles. Although it appears that St Peter
engaged in hypocritical behavior upon the arrival of the Jewish Christians from Jerusalem, some fathers (e.g., St John Chrysostom and St
Jerome) minimize any real conflict between the two apostles and rather
emphasize how St Peter attempted in a humble and loving manner
to address a very delicate situation with the Jewish Christian visitors
while at the same time consciously creating an opportunity for St Paul

[1]Kristoffer Nyrop, *The Kiss and Its History*, trans. W. F. Harvey (New York: E. P.
Dutton and Co., 1902), 173. This charming book provides a fascinating look at the
kiss through history.

to publically correct him and thereby teach all who were present. For example, St John Chrysostom commenting on this incident states:

> The Apostles ... permitted circumcision at Jerusalem, an abrupt severance from the law not being practicable; but when they came to Antioch, they no longer continued this observance, but lived indiscriminately with the believing Gentiles which thing Peter also was at that time doing. But when some came from Jerusalem who had heard the doctrine he delivered there, he no longer did so fearing to perplex them, but he changed his course, with two objects secretly in view, both to avoid offending those Jews, and to give Paul a reasonable pretext for rebuking him.[2]

Others (e.g., St Augustine) have been more censorious of the Apostle Peter's behavior, discerning weakness and hypocrisy on his part:

> Peter ... when he came to Antioch, was rebuked by Paul not because he observed the Jewish custom in which he was born and reared, although he did not observe it among the Gentiles, but because he wanted to impose it on the Gentiles ... after seeing certain persons come from James ... the head of the church in Jerusalem. It was therefore in fear of those who still thought that salvation resided in these observances that Peter separated himself from the Gentiles and pretended to consent in imposing those burdens of servitude on the Gentiles.[3]

Regardless of the specific motives underlying the actions of the two apostles in this incident, the Church's Tradition has most emphatically confirmed the ultimate resolution of their conflict in its iconography (see plate 13). It is the reconciliation between these princes of the apostles and this resolution's expression through the sense of touch that are the subjects of this reflection. The humility and ultimately the deep fraternal love St Peter demonstrated through his patient acceptance of St Paul's public reproof may be of greater and more fundamental

---

[2]St John Chrysostom, *Commentary on Galatians* (NPNF[1] 13:18–19).
[3]St Augustine, in ACCS:NT 8:27.

significance than the actual issues underlying their disagreement. Scriptural evidence corroborating the healing in the apostles' relationship—which is so vividly portrayed in the icon showing their kiss of peace—is also presented in the way in which St Peter refers to his fellow apostle in his Second Epistle as "our beloved [*agapētos*, Greek] brother Paul" (2 Pet 3.15).

A kiss on both cheeks is still a common form of greeting in many cultures. Whatever its primary significance in pagan Rome, the early Christians transformed the meaning of this ancient greeting. Both Sts Peter and Paul used a similar final greeting in their Epistles: "Greet one another with a holy kiss" (*philōmati hagiō*, Greek; see Rom 16.16; 1 Cor 16.20; 1 Thess 5.26) or with a "kiss of love" (*philōmati agapēs*, Greek; 1 Pet 5.14). At least as early as the third century, the kiss of peace was exchanged between persons within the community of the faithful as a formal part of liturgical worship.[4] In the early Church, great care was taken during the liturgy, with the process being supervised by the diaconate, to create an orderly assembly of the faithful by rank and gender. In an Easter homily of the early fifth century, St Augustine mentions the "holy kiss" of Christians that was exchanged at the Divine Liturgy as being from mouth to mouth rather than mouth to cheek, which may explain the scrupulous separation of genders during the liturgy at that time, to avoid unseemly kissing between men and women. "Christians kiss one another with a holy kiss. It's a sign of peace; what is indicated by the lips should happen in the conscience; that is, just as your lips approach the lips of your brothers or sisters, so your heart should not be withdrawn from theirs."[5] In preparing the faithful to receive the Eucharist, after dismissing the catechumens near the beginning of the second portion of the Divine Liturgy, the deacon serving at the altar would say, "Let no one have any quarrel against another; let

[4]See Hippolytus, *Apostolic Tradition* 18.4 (PPS 54:124), a third century Roman text; cf. *Apostolic Constitutions* 2.7.57 (ANF 7:422), a fourth century Syrian text.

[5]St Augustine, Sermon 227, in St Augustine, *Sermons: On the Liturgical Seasons*, trans. Edmund Hill, *The Works of Saint Augustine: A Translation for the 21st Century*, Part III—Sermons, Vol. 6 (New Rochelle, NY: New City Press, 1993), 255.

no one come in hypocrisy."[6] The tangible seal of this precommunion reconciliation was in the form of exchanging a kiss: "Let the men give the men, and the women give the women, the Lord's kiss. But let no one do it with deceit, as Judas betrayed the Lord with a kiss."[7] By the eighth century in the patriarchal Divine Liturgy celebrated in the great church of Hagia Sophia in Constantinople, the holy kiss was initiated immediately before reciting the creed when the patriarch turned to the faithful and said, "Peace to all." The archdeacon then followed with the injunction to share the peace, "Let us love one another," and then, as described in the earlier *Apostolic Constitutions*, the kiss of peace was exchanged among those present.[8]

It is interesting to note that the Greek word for "kiss," *to philōma*, is closely aligned with the verb *phileō*, which means "love," "have affection for," or "like." Indeed, a secondary meaning of the verb *phileō* is to demonstrate affection or love in a special way by *kissing* another person.[9] This exchange of peace before reciting the Creed has persisted within the Divine Liturgy in the form of the holy kiss that is shared between clergy serving at the altar, and in some Orthodox Christian jurisdictions the practice has been revived to varying degrees among the laity. Why was this seemingly trivial action of such importance that it merited being included in one of the earliest Christian descriptions of the eucharistic celebration, and then of such importance that the practice endured through the centuries? What is the significance of its being located in the Liturgy immediately before the recitation of the Creed?

It may be nearly impossible for modern sensibilities to conceive of how a kiss might convey a deep, intimate form of love without erotic overtones. But this is precisely what the early Church strove to do, consciously taking measures to separate the erotic quality from the

[6] *Apostolic Constitutions* 2.7.57 (ANF 7:422).

[7] Ibid.

[8] St Germanus of Constantinople, *On the Divine Liturgy*, trans. and ed. Paul Meyendorff. PPS 8 (Crestwood, NY: St Vladimir's Press, 1984), introduction p. 22.

[9] William F. Arndt and F. W. Gingrich, *A Greek-English Lexicon of the New Testament and Other Early Christian Literature* (Chicago: University of Chicago Press, 1957), 866–67.

encounter while still emphasizing the crucial sacramental character of physical contact shared as a kiss between persons. Faith transformed this ancient form of greeting into an ineffable exchange of self-sacrificial love, actualizing the reconciliation which must occur before individual Christians could ascend into a higher union as members of the one body. Thus, the timing in the liturgy is crucial. We must first be fully reconciled with one another before we can honestly proclaim our faith in the One who would commune with us and heal us in his body and blood. In this mystery, Christians were offered at every liturgy the opportunity to reverse the act of Judas, whose kiss of friendship and love had degenerated into a means of betrayal and an expression of the worst of the passions (Lk 22.47–48).

For the Christian, a holy kiss in the perfection of its simplicity is the tangible demonstration of one's fervent love for God in one's neighbor that has been made possible through the incarnation of his divine Word. The greater humility expressed in the kiss, the greater the love. In Luke's Gospel, the sinful woman's love was materially manifested as she washed Christ's feet with her tears, anointed them with myrrh, and kissed them (Lk 7.37ff.). Her veneration through her kisses of the only One who could heal her was a sacrament of reconciliation that prefigured the later kiss of peace of the faithful and the healing encounter present within the kiss of an icon. In one of St John Chrysostom's prayers before communion, he reminds each one of us who prepare to approach the chalice of the great humility of the harlot as she touched Christ's feet with her lips and how far we fall short of it: "And as you did not cast out the harlot, a sinner like me, who came and touched you, so have compassion on me the sinner who now comes to touch you. And as you did not abhor the kiss of her sinful and unclean mouth, do not abhor my mouth, more stained and unclean than hers, nor my sordid and unclean and shameless lips, nor my more unclean tongue."[10]

What are the deeper implications of engaging in this special form of contact? St Maximus the Confessor, in his *Centuries on Love*, offers profound insights into the depth of love and reconciliation manifested in

[10]St John Chrysostom, "Prayer Before Communion," in *Daily Prayers*, 84.

the icon of Sts Peter and Paul exchanging the kiss of peace: "If we detect any trace of hatred in our hearts against any man whatsoever for committing any fault, we are utterly estranged from love for God, since love for God absolutely precludes us from hating any man. . . . Blessed is he who can love all men equally."[11] Recognizing our frailty, Saint Maximus urges us to at least make a beginning in this most basic struggle with our passions: "Strive as hard as you can to love every man. If you cannot yet do this, at least do not hate anybody."[12] The kiss of peace exchanged by the faithful in preparation for receiving the body and blood of Christ is an expression of absolute renunciation of hatred and a complete, sincere turning in all humility toward love. But, it cannot be merely an intellectual assent; the whole person must be engaged, one *prosōpon*[13] touching another, using some of the most sensitive points of contact in the body, the lips of the mouth.[14] The same lips that may have uttered curses and blasphemies or wounded others through angry words and gossip must now become the vehicles of expressing the self-sacrificial love of the disciple of the Crucified One. "A new commandment I give to you, that you love one another; just as I have loved you, so must you also love one another. By this, all will know that you are my disciples, if you have love for one another" (Jn 13.34–35, author's translation). St Maximus describes the cost of such love for one's neighbor:

[11]St Maximus the Confessor, *Four Hundred Texts on Love* 1.15, 17, in *Philokalia* 2:54.

[12]St Maximus the Confessor, *Four Hundred Texts on Love* 4.82, in *Philokalia* 2:111.

[13]*Prosōpon* in Greek means "face," hence, the person behind the face.

[14]In classic experiments during the 1930s, Wilder Penfield used electrical stimulation of the surface of the brain to map the somatosensory and motor cortex. He generated a peculiar homunculus, or "little human," image or map of sensory and motor functions distributed in the cortex that was distorted as it emphasized the particularly rich sensory input coming from certain areas, including the lips and oral cavity (W. Penfield and E. Boldrey, "Somatic Motor and Sensory Representation in the Cerebral Cortex of Man as Studied by Electrical Stimulation," *Brain Journal* 60 [1937]: 389–443). Many of Penfield's observations, including the prominent representation of the lips in the somatosensory cortex, have been confirmed using newer research techniques (e.g., B. T. Nguyen et al., "Face Representation in the Human Primary Somatosensory Cortex," *Neuroscience Research* 50 [2004]: 227–32).

He who loves Christ is bound to imitate Him to the best of his ability. Christ, for example, was always conferring blessings on people; He was long-suffering when they were ungrateful and blasphemed Him; and when they beat Him and put Him to death, He endured it, imputing no evil at all to anyone. These are the three acts which manifest love for one's neighbor. . . . Only God is good by nature, and only he who imitates God is good in will and purpose. For it is the intention of such a person to unite the wicked to Him who is good by nature, so that they too may become good. That is why, though reviled by them, he blesses; persecuted, he endures; vilified, he supplicates; put to death, he prays for them. He does everything so as not to lapse from *the purpose of love, which is God Himself.*[15]

Even though historically the kiss of peace was exchanged between persons of similar rank and gender, by virtue of the power of the humble love transmitted through such tender contact and shared in the common cup, it transcends every barrier between human persons: race, nationality, gender, education, social class, and even ego. What the union of *Eros* lacks, the kiss of peace completes and extends to all persons. Herein lies the power of a kiss: if administered as the kiss of peace, it becomes a channel by which the healing grace of God can flow between persons, creating a truly sanctified unity.

[15]St Maximos the Confessor, *Four Hundred Texts on Love* 4.55, 90, in *Philokalia* 2:107, 111–12 (author's emphasis).

Plate 14

CHAPTER 13

The Divine Embrace in Death

Today you will be with me in paradise.

—Luke 23.43

THROUGHOUT RECORDED HISTORY, we know that human beings have struggled with the inevitability of death. The great world religions, including materialistic atheism in our own time, have had to address the very long shadow cast by human suffering and mortality over the cultures in which they have arisen. Indeed, one might judge the "success" or truth of a given religion by how well it responds to this omnipresent reality of human experience. Inherent within the responses given by the various religions to the imperatives of human suffering and mortality are the answers they offer to the question of what happens after death. It is here that Christianity departs radically and most fundamentally from other religions. Indeed, to the outside observer or curious academic, Christianity is categorized as a monotheistic religion arising out of Judaism. And yet, by this simple assertion of the Crucified One to the good thief—"Today you will be with me in paradise"— religious categories are overthrown and have no relevance whatsoever. The profound statement quoted above by the dying Jewish messiah to a criminal dying beside him changes everything. The transformation of a human soul at the eleventh hour[1] through the proximity of contact with the Word-Made-Flesh is a foretaste, a prophetic acknowledgement, of Christ's descent into Hades and victory over death. When by grace the good thief witnesses to the Truth being crucified beside him, this most unlikely evangelist cooperates with the

[1]Cf. Mt 20.1–16. This recognition of Christ by the good thief apparently reached its full maturity during the course of the crucifixion, since both thieves were noted to rail at Christ initially (cf. Mk 15.32).

Lord in making the first proclamation of the destruction of death by death. In his acceptance of his suffering and unreserved recognition of the innocence of Christ (Lk 23.41), he glorifies God and transforms his execution as a criminal into the witness or martyrdom of a faithful servant of the Lord. He receives the full payment, the denarius of salvation, in that very short moment of intense labor in the vineyard (Mt 20.1–16), a payment that defies all human logic but fulfills the mercy and justice of the God who is Love. Clearly, by any estimate he should have been the least likely candidate to be a disciple, and yet he fills the place of all those who had fled at the arrest of their Master.

By stating to the thief, "Today you will be with me in paradise" (Lk 23.43), the Lord, who is still hanging on the cross, affirms the miraculous and transformative reality of humble faith. The thief, in that incomprehensible moment, has the scales drop from his eyes, and, like the three disciples on the mount of transfiguration, he witnesses the Lord of Glory hanging from the tree. In his recognition of Christ, all the barriers of self—the passions, which had so dominated his existence—have been removed to reveal the Paradise hanging beside him. This is the extraordinary miracle being offered to each person who can call upon the name of the Lord, even at the eleventh hour of one's earthly existence.

But what of another witness who was standing at the foot of the cross—a witness who quite literally carried the Lord of Glory within her own womb, who nursed him at her breast, who held and comforted the Creator and Sustainer of the universe in her arms? Her epiphany of the incarnate Lord came through the loving embrace between mother and child. Unlike the thief, hers was a proximity extending over a lifetime, an ineffable intimacy nurtured and continually strengthened through an ever-deepening relationship between persons. This was no eleventh hour conversion on the part of the one who said *yes* at the annunciation. Like the thief, she also received the denarius of salvation, and yet so much more!

In St John the Theologian's Gospel, the evangelist records the extraordinary exchange of the crucified Son of the Virgin with his mother and the disciple whom he loved. When he blesses a new relationship between his mother and his disciple, he, in effect, transfers her motherhood to all his disciples, the Church, and thus she becomes the mother of a new creation in her Son. If the good thief by faith can be transported to paradise in a moment, what then can be said of the Virgin, from whom the Word of God acquired his humanity and a renewed humanity received its mother?

For the Church, the Theotokos is the ultimate model of the encounter between the human person and God. The icon of the dormition of the Theotokos (see plate 14) emphatically affirms that, like all her children, the Mother of God, in her mortal human nature, could not avoid the encounter with death. Rather than the eleventh-hour transfiguration experienced by the good thief, the Virgin's life and death are understood within the Church's Tradition to exemplify the perfect union between the human soul and the divine that occurs as the never-ending process of deification, or *theosis*, beginning to live by grace in the kingdom of God even during this life. From the miraculous circumstances of her conception; her early life in the Jerusalem temple;[2] her complete and unconditional acceptance of the Word who would be made flesh within her womb; and her witness to the crucifixion, death, and resurrection of her Son in the Gospel accounts, her life was increasingly seen by the Church fathers as the template for the life in Christ. Not only is this to be fully consummated at death, but also it may even be experienced on this side of the grave by the grace of the Holy Spirit within the sacramental life of the Church.

The christological controversies that served as catalysts for the seven great ecumenical councils led to the Church's answer to Christ's question: "Who do you say that I am?" (Mk 8.29). As the Church refined its understanding of the nature of the God-Man, it was inevitable that his relationship to his mother would also be examined in greater detail

[2]Much of the Virgin Mary's life and the circumstances of her death are shrouded in mystery, with relatively little mention made of her in the Gospel accounts. The second-century *Protoevangelium (or Infancy Gospel) of St James* (for the text, see M. R. James, *The Apocryphal New Testament* [London: Oxford University Press, 1966], 38–49), provides many details of her early life, but later Fathers of the Church still puzzled over the relative paucity of written accounts regarding her death.

within the collective reflection of the faithful. The fruit growing out of this reflection was centered on the meaning of her falling asleep in death, her dormition. How could it be possible for the one who bore the very Source of life within her womb to remain in the grave, experiencing corruption?

As noted in chapter 1, the Virgin's pivotal role as the *second Eve* in the healing transformation of human nature damaged by the sin of the first Eve was already recognized by such Church fathers as St Irenaeus as early as the second century. This recognition combined with the sifting of a very long oral tradition resulted by the late sixth to early seventh centuries in the establishment and celebration of the solemn Feast of her Dormition throughout the Christian Roman empire. With the addition of this feast to the Church calendar, later Church fathers began to offer rhetorical homage to Mary as the Theotokos in the form of sermons in honor of the Feast of her Dormition. Her death, after all, represented the completion of her mission as the second Eve. By grace, she experienced a reciprocal transformation, the deification of her humanity (and by extension, all human nature) as she offered her humanity to the divine presence within her womb. In effect, her life and death represent the fullest flowering of the hope of all Christians: union with God in *theōsis*. In contrast to the good thief, the second Eve, in the entirety of her life and death, is the confirmation of the very real possibility of an ever-expanding relationship between creature and Creator that transcends any conceivable earthly human hope, which can begin in this life well before the eleventh hour. St Andrew of Crete (+740), in the introductory remarks to his *First Homily on the Dormition of the Theotokos*, clearly expresses his hesitation to approach such a great mystery when he says, "One ought to avoid saying the unsayable by keeping a deep silence."[3]

Certain elements of the traditional account of the Virgin's falling asleep are essential to understand from the Eastern Church's perspective: she aged, declined in health, and physically died. The Church also insists

---

[3]St Andrew of Crete, *On the Dormition of Our Most Holy Lady, the Mother of God*, Homily 1.1, in *On the Dormition of Mary: Early Patristic Homilies*, trans. Brian E. Daley, PPS 18 (Crestwood, NY: St Vladimir's Seminary Press, 1998), 103.

that after death, like her Son, she experienced bodily resurrection and assumption into the kingdom. As the mother of a new and restored humanity, her service as intercessor, advocate, and protectress for her children is a reflection of her special relationship with her Son and is a reality felt and experienced by many Christians. The icon (plate 14) presents other elements of the tradition concerning her death. Before she died she was given foreknowledge through an angelic announcement (another annunciation) of her impending death in three days. Miraculously, the apostles, including St Paul but excluding St Thomas, were transported to her deathbed to witness her departure from this life. The absence of the doubting disciple made it possible for him to later confirm, when he did arrive a few days later, that her tomb was empty. However, the key element of the icon that is outlined within the *mandorla*, or bright aureole in the center of the image, is the appearance of her Son in his glory with the angels receiving his mother's soul into his arms.

The recognition that this woman who had carried within her body the fullness of the Godhead was now being embraced in death by her eternal Son challenged those gifted with great rhetorical skills to even begin, in some paltry sense, to approach this ineffable mystery. Pondering what must have been on the minds of the angels who were present at her passing from this life, St Modestus of Jerusalem (+634) mused, "She contained the uncontainable one, she bore the fire of divinity without being singed, she gave birth to the maker of all, she cradled in her arms him who carries the universe in his hand, she fondled him 'who looks down on the earth and makes it to tremble' (Ps 103:32 [LXX]), she fed him 'who gives food to all flesh' (Ps 135:25 [LXX])."[4] He goes on to observe that the mission of the Theotokos "was to become, on earth, God's bridge beyond this universe . . . through her, he has made known to us the way to ascend to him by right faith, and by the good life that leads to heaven."[5]

A recurring theme of the Fathers in their homilies on the dormition is the incomprehensible wedding of the natural with the supernatural,

[4]St Modestus of Jerusalem, *An Encomium on the Dormition of Our Most Holy Lady, Mary, Mother of God, and Ever-Virgin* 8, in *On the Dormition of Mary*, 93.

[5]*An Encomium on the Dormition* 9, ibid., 94.

the material with the immaterial, that occurred within her womb: "He has shown forth from you in our substance on earth,"[6] and "The most brilliant of God's self-revelation, the divine formation of Jesus as one like us, took place by an unprecedented and indescribable act of God's providence, in the workshop of a virgin's human nature."[7] In contemplating the significance of carrying the incorruptible Word of God in her womb, St Andrew of Crete draws the logical conclusion that such intimate contact between divinity and humanity could not help but have a profound, transformative effect on the essence of human nature touched by the divine. How could she who bore the Incorruptible One suffer corruption after death?

> It is truly a new spectacle, never before conceived of: a woman who surpasses the heavens in purity of nature enters the holy tabernacle of the heavenly sanctuary; a virgin, who surpasses the very nature of the Seraphim by the miracle of giving birth to God, draws near to God, the first of natures and begetter of all things; a mother, who has brought forth life itself, produces an ending of her own life to match that of her Son. It is a miracle worthy both of God and of our faith! For as her womb was not corrupted in giving birth, so her flesh did not perish in dying. . . . The child put corruption to flight, and the tomb did not admit of corruption—for it has no claim on holy things.[8]

The condescension of God in the incarnation of the Word was brought to perfection in the relationship between human mother and divine Child, which is depicted in the *Eleousa* icon of the Theotokos and Child (see plate 2). Not only does she give her humanity to God, but also she gives her emphatic *yes* to God's desire to physically touch his creatures. But the incredible aspect of this relationship is the way in which the divine touch is manifested. In the extraordinary humility that is the essence of the divine, Love comes to embrace his creation as an infant seeking out the caresses of his mother. The Virgin is the

---

[6] *An Encomium on the Dormition* 10, ibid., 95.
[7] St Andrew of Crete, *On the Dormition*, Homily 1.1, ibid., 103.
[8] St Andrew of Crete, *On the Dormition*, Homily 1.6, ibid., 110.

ambassador of a fallen creation to its Creator, who comes in all the vulnerability of a child, seeking reconciliation with his cosmos through the reassurance of a mother's touch. God's kiss of peace for his creation begins with the kiss between a baby and his mother. St Andrew, in wonder at this relationship between the Creator and the second Eve, exclaims, "She is the great world in miniature, the world containing him who brought the world from nothingness into being, that it might be the messenger of his own greatness."[9] Perhaps there is nothing more irresistible to the hardest of human hearts than to witness the expression on a child's face pressed cheek-to-cheek with its mother, carrying a mixture of every human emotion untainted by the passions. He who said, "Unless you change and become as little children" (Mt 18.3) was really calling us to become like him, the Child, par excellence.

In the icon of the dormition, the relationship between Son and mother, between Creator and creature, as a circle is closed and perfected. Now the Son comes in his glory with his angels and receives his mother's soul, tenderly embracing her to himself. St Germanus of Constantinople (+c.740) imagines the words spoken by the Son to his mother at this moment of fulfillment:

> When you lived in the world of corruptible things, I revealed my power to you in visions; now that you are passing from that life, I will show myself to you face to face. Give the earth what belongs to it, without anxiety. Your body belongs to me, and since the ends of the earth are in my hand, no one can take anything from me. Entrust your body to me, just as I placed my divinity trustingly in your womb. Your soul, full of divine power, will see the glory of my Father. Your immaculate body will see the glory of his only Son. Your pure spirit will see the glory of the all-holy Spirit.[10]

In this imagined conversation between Christ and his mother, who is the quintessential model of the human person seeking union with the

---

[9]St Andrew of Crete, *On the Dormition*, Homily 2.15, ibid., 133.

[10]St Germanus of Constantinople, *An Encomium on the Holy and Venerable Dormition of our Most Glorious Lady, the Mother of God and Ever-Virgin Mary*, Homily 2.2, ibid., 171.

divine, St Germanus presents a Trinitarian vision of *theōsis* in which the three aspects of the person—body, soul, and spirit—fully encounter God as a community of love.

Reflecting on the extraordinary mercy and loving condescension of God shown to all humanity through the Virgin Mary, St Andrew of Crete exclaims, "O provider of life, life of the living, part of the cause of our life! O holy one, holier than all the saints, supremely holy treasury of all that makes us holy! O woman *who as one individual*, without division or dissolution, united humanity to God!"[11] St Andrew goes on to explain how the action, the *yes*, of this one woman has initiated a new and transformed relationship between the Creator and his creation: "It is no less accurate to say: he became human in order to make you wholly divine in the Spirit, to consume the worse in the better, to raise you up to himself from the earth and to enthrone you among your ancestors. Be drawn up to him, always, in your way of life and in your pure contemplation; live out a pattern of holy words and habits; see God, as far as that is possible, and let him see you."[12] And one could even add "let him touch you," since his assumption of our humanity from his virgin mother has established an indissoluble bond between the material and the immaterial, between human nature deified and divine love.

> Through her, our age-old war against our creator has come to an end. Through her, our reconciliation with him has been forged, peace and grace have been bestowed on us, human beings join with the chorus of angels, and we who were once without honor have now been made children of God. From her, we have plucked the grape of life; from her we have harvested the flower of incorruptibility. She has become the mediator of all good things for us. In her, God has become human and the human being God![13]

[11]St Andrew of Crete, *On the Dormition*, Homily 3.15, ibid., 149 (author's emphasis).

[12]Ibid., 150.

[13]St John of Damascus, *On the Holy and Glorious Dormition and Transformation of our Lady Mary, Mother of God and Ever-Virgin*, Homily 2.16, ibid., 220.

The *Telos* of Touch

And the Word became flesh and dwelt among us, and we observed his glory, glory as of the only begotten of the Father, full of grace and truth.
—John 1.14 (author's translation)

I T HAS BEEN THE THESIS of this small volume, expressed both in the icons presented and the accompanying reflections, that *the Word became flesh* so that he might touch and be touched by his creation. The Ineffable One became tangible so that he might communicate where words fail. Isolation is antithetical to love, and touch (or contact) in a material universe is antithetical to isolation. For God, who is the very essence of love, not to desire an intimate relationship with his isolated and wounded creatures is incomprehensible. If Love as pure spirit, pure other, desires to heal, to repair, the brokenness of his creation, how else could this be achieved other than by assuming the material nature of his creation so that intimate contact could be made?

The sense of touch makes it possible to encounter mystery. But all of the senses, and perhaps especially touch, represent a two-edged sword. Those very instruments given to us by God can as easily be our downfall as our salvation. The passible nature of the fallen human person, so easily subject to the passions, has resulted in a distortion of our senses. Like Adam and Eve in the garden of Eden, we so often reach out and touch with a selfish, autonomous desire to possess and control rather than in obedience, waiting upon God, so that we might be touched and healed in the mystery of communion.

From the beginning of God's self-revelation to his creatures he has sought us out and, whenever possible, invited us to approach and touch. This was the foundation of his relationship with his servant

Moses, who eventually became known as the friend of God (Ex 33.11). But the foundation of that friendship was also critically dependent on Moses' removing his sandals, signifying the passions that are a barrier to close intimate contact with God. Thus, in plate 1 the burning bush icon in many ways sums up the whole content of this book. It not only speaks directly to the conditions that are foundational to the journey of *theōsis*—cleansing the soul of the passions and acquiring the virtues, especially humility—but it also gives powerful testimony to the nature of the union between creature and Creator at its very heart. In the Church's Tradition, it has been seen not only as a type of the incarnation of our Lord—the Virgin Mary bears God within her womb and is not consumed by the divine presence—but also as a type of each communing member of the body of Christ. Indeed, the Church fathers emphasize the various forms of touching Christ that are documented in the Gospels only to draw back in reverent awe when considering the bold act of the believer who approaches the chalice:

> Open for me the depth of your love, and receive me as I draw near and touch you, as did the harlot and the woman with the issue of blood. The latter only touched the hem of your garment, and she immediately received healing, while the former, clinging to your pure feet, obtained forgiveness of her sins. *But may I, the miserable one, be not consumed, by daring to receive your whole body.*[1]

Perhaps another way to summarize the meaning of the different icons and reflections presented in this book is to recognize that Christ as the incarnate Word of God sought us out in every aspect of our humanity, making himself a part of his own created order for one ultimate purpose: that there may be no barrier preventing our full communion with the divine. Each of the healing miracles presented—the holy *eros* of Sts Joachim and Anna, the divine baptizing of the waters of the world, the humble washing of each disciple's feet, the horrors of the crucifixion and torture of God, the powerful grasp and rescue of those

---

[1]St John of Damascus, "Prayer Before Communion," in *Daily Prayers for Orthodox Christians: The Synekdemos*, 94 (author's emphasis).

in Hades by the conqueror of death, the revelation in the breaking of the bread at Emmaus, the doubter's touch turned to faith, and the kiss of peace so essential to the unity of the body of Christ—is a reflection of Christ's transformation of the sensual into healing elements of the kingdom of God. The bookends for these tangible encounters with the divine, of course, are the icons of the Theotokos and Child and the dormition of the Theotokos, in which the entire intervention of God in his creation is circumscribed. God is encountered most intimately at the beginning of life within the loving caresses and kisses of a mother and child and, at the end of life, when entering through the portal of eternity, within the caresses of his love unto ages of ages. Amen.

> In truth, then, God became a man and provided another beginning, a second nativity, for human nature, which, through the vehicle of suffering, ends in the pleasure of the life to come.[2]

---

[2]St Maximus the Confessor, *Ad Thalassium 61*, in *On the Cosmic Mystery of Jesus Christ*, trans. Paul M. Blowers and Robert Louis Wilken, PPS 25 (Crestwood, NY: St Vladimir's Seminary Press, 2003), 135.

Acknowledgments

I N ADDITION TO the support and initial guidance of Fr Roman Braga, the creation of this book has been blessed by the efforts and prayers of several individuals, some of whom I particularly want to thank and acknowledge here. A nun-iconographer and member of the sisterhood of Holy Dormition Monastery, Rives Junction, Michigan, painted the icons that have inspired the reflections presented in each of the chapters of the book. Her remarkable efforts could not have been accomplished without the support of Mother Gabriella, the abbess of Holy Dormition Monastery, and of her fellow nuns. Fr Ian Pac-Urar prepared the high-resolution photographs of each of the icons, a task that was at times challenging, as some of the icons form part of the interior decoration of the monastery church. Nicholas Simon very generously provided the photograph of Fr Roman that is presented in the dedication. Fr John Konkle, the priest serving the monastic community, very kindly reviewed the manuscript and provided many helpful and insightful suggestions for its improvement. I am also very grateful to Donna Kehoe for her careful reading and editing of the manuscript. Finally, I am thankful to my wife, Jane, who provided a thoughtful review of the manuscript in our shared desire to honor Fr Roman.

Abbreviations

ACCS   Ancient Christian Commentary on Scripture. 29 vols. Downers Grove, IL: InterVarsity Press, 1998–2010.

ANF   The Ante-Nicene Fathers. Edited by Alexander Roberts and James Donaldson. 10 vols. Buffalo, 1885–96. Reprint, Peabody, MA: Hendrickson, 1994.

FOTC   The Fathers of the Church: A New Translation. Washington, DC: The Catholic University of America, 1947–

LCL   Loeb Classical Library. Cambridge, MA: Harvard University Press, 1911–

NPNF¹   *The Nicene and Post-Nicene Fathers*, Series 1. Edited by Philip Schaff. 14 vols. New York, 1886–89. Reprint, Peabody, MA: Hendrickson, 1994.

NPNF²   *The Nicene and Post-Nicene Fathers*, Series 2. Edited by Philip Schaff and Henry Wace. 14 vols. New York, 1890. Reprint, Peabody, MA: Hendrickson, 1994.

Philokalia   *Philokalia: The Complete Text.* Edited by G. E. H. Palmer, Philip Sherrard, and Kallistos Ware. 4 vols. London: Faber & Faber, 1979–95.

PPS   Popular Patristics Series. Yonkers, NY: St Vladimir's Seminary Press, 1996–

Bibliography

Church Fathers and Other Primary Texts Cited

Ambrose, *Concerning Repentance*, in NPNF² 10:329–59.

_____. *On the Holy Spirit.* In NPNF² 10:91–158.

_____. *Letter 41.* In NPNF² 10:445–50.

_____. *Letter 63.* In NPNF² 10:457–73.

_____. *On Virginity*, 2nd ed. Trans. Daniel Callam. Peregrina Translations Series 7. Toronto: Peregrina, 1980.

Andrew of Crete. *On the Dormition of Our Most Holy Lady, the Mother of God,* Homily 1–3. In PPS 18:103–52.

Apostolic Constitutions. In ANF 7:387–505.

Athanasius. *On the Incarnation.* A Religious of C.S.M.V. PPS 3. Crestwood, NY: St Vladimir's Seminary Press, 1993 [1st ed. 1944].

_____. *On the Incarnation: Greek Original and English Translation.* Trans. John Behr. PPS 44a. Crestwood, NY: St Vladimir's Seminary Press, 2011.

Augustine. *The City of God.* In NPNF¹ 2:1–511.

_____. *On Genesis: A Refutation of the Manichees Unfinished Literal Commentary on Genesis, the Literal Meaning of Genesis.* Trans. Edmund Hill. *The Works of Augustine: A Translation for the 21st Century,* Part 1, Vol. 13. Hyde Park, NY: New City Press, 2002.

_____. *Lectures or Tractates on the Gospel According to St John.* In NPNF¹ 7:1–452.

_____. *Sermons: On the Liturgical Seasons.* Trans. Edmund Hill, *The Works of Saint Augustine: A Translation for the 21st Century,* Part III—Sermons, Vol. 6. New Rochelle, NY: New City Press, 1993.

Basil the Great. *The Hexaemeron.* In NPNF² 8:52–107.

_____. *On the Human Condition.* Trans. Sr Nonna Harrison. PPS 30. Crestwood, NY: St Vladimir's Seminary Press, 2005.

Daily Prayers for Orthodox Christians: The Synekdemos. Ed. N. Michael Vaporis. Brookline, MA: Holy Cross Orthodox Press, 1986.

Diadochus of Photiki. *On Spiritual Knowledge and Discernment: One Hunred Texts.* In *Philokalia* 1:252–96.

Ephrem the Syrian. *Hymns on Paradise.* Trans. Sebastian Brock. PPS 10. Crestwood, NY: St Vladimir's Seminary Press, 1990.

_____. *Saint Ephrem's Commentary on Tatian's Diatessaron: An English Translation of Chester Beatty Syriac MS 709.* Trans. Carmel McCarthy. Oxford: Oxford University Press, 1993.

Eusebius of Caesarea. *Ecclesiastical History,* Vol. 2. LCL 265.

Evagrius the Solitary. *On Prayer: One Hundred and Fifty-Three Texts.* In *Philokalia* 1:55–71.

Germanus of Constantinople. *On the Divine Liturgy.* Trans. Paul Meyendorff. PPS 8. Crestwood, NY: St Vladimir's Press, 1984.

_____. *An Encomium on the Holy and Venerable Dormition of our Most Glorious Lady, the Mother of God and Ever-Virgin Mary.* Homily 2. In PPS 18:169–81.

Greek Orthodox Holy Week and Easter Services. Trans. Fr George L. Papadeas. South Daytona, FL: Patmos Press, 1996.

Gregory the Great. *Gregory the Great: Forty Gospel Homilies.* Trans. David Hurst. Cistercian Studies 126. Collegeville, MN: Cistercian Publications, 1990.

Gregory Nazianzus. *Oration 43, Panegyric on St Basil.* NPNF² 7:395–422.

_____. *The Second Oration on Easter.* In NPNF² 7:422–34.

Gregory of Nyssa. *Address on Religious Instruction.* In *Christology of the Later Fathers.* Ed. Edward Rochie Hardy and Cyril C. Richardson. Pp. 268–325. Philadelphia: Westminster Press, 1977.

Hippolytus. *On the Apostolic Tradition,* 2nd ed. Trans. Alastair Stewart. PPS 54. Yonkers, NY: St Vladimir's Seminary Press, 2015.

_____. *The Discourse on the Holy Theophany.* In ANF 5:234–37.

Ignatius of Antioch. *Ignatius of Antioch: The Letters.* Trans. Alastair Stewart. PPS 49. Yonkers, NY: St Vladimir's Seminary Press, 2013.

Irenaeus. *Against Heresies.* In ANF 1:315–567.

Isaac of Syria. *Ascetical Homilies of Saint Isaac the Syrian.* Boston, MA: Holy Transfiguration Monastery, 1984.

Jerome. *The Dialogue Against the Luciferians.* NPNF² 6:319–34.

John Chrysostom. *Commentary on Galatians*. In NPNF¹ 13:1–48.

_____. *The Homilies of St John Chrysostom on the Gospel of St John*. In NPNF¹ 14:1–334.

_____. *The Homilies of St John Chrysostom on the Gospel of St Matthew*. In NPNF¹ 10:1–534.

_____. *Homilies on First Corinthians*. In NPNF¹ 12:1–269.

_____. *On Marriage and Family Life*. Trans. Catherine P. Roth and David Anderson. PPS 7. Crestwood, NY: St Vladimir's Seminary Press, 1991.

John Climacus. *The Ladder of Divine Ascent*. Trans. Colm Luibheid and Norman Russell. Mahwah, NJ: Paulist Press, 1982.

John of Damascus. *An Exact Exposition of the Orthodox Faith*. In NPNF² 9:1b–101b.

_____. *On the Holy and Glorious Dormition and Transformation of our Lady Mary, Mother of God and Ever-Virgin*. Homily 2. In *On the Dormition of Mary: Early Patristic Homilies*. Trans. Brian E. Daly. PPS 18. Crestwood, NY: St Vladimir's Press, 1997; pp. 203–223.

Maximus the Confessor. *On the Cosmic Mystery of Jesus Christ*. Trans. Paul M. Blowers and Robert L. Wilken. PPS 25. Crestwood, NY: St Vladimir's Seminary Press, 2003.

_____. *Four Hundred Texts on Love*. In *Philokalia* 2:52–113.

Modestus of Jerusalem, *An Encomium on the Dormition of Our Most Holy Lady, Mary, Mother of God, and Ever-Virgin*. In PPS 18:83–102.

Peter Chrysologus. *Saint Peter Chrysologus: Selected Sermons and Saint Valerian: Homilies*. Trans. George E. Ganns. FOTC 17. Washington, DC: The Catholic University of America, 1953.

Protoevangelium of St James. In *The Apocryphal New Testament*. Ed. M. R. James. Pp. 38–49. London: Oxford University Press, 1966.

Romanus the Melodist. *On the Life of Christ: Kontakia*, Trans. Ephrem Lash. San Francisco: HarperCollins Publishers, 1995.

Simeon the New Theologian. *One Hundred and Fifty-Three Practical and Theological Texts*. In *Philokalia* 4:25–66.

Tertullian. *Against Marcion*. In ANF 3:271–474.

Theophylact. *The Explanation by Blessed Theophylact of the Holy Gospel According to John*. Trans. Fr Christopher Stade. House Springs, MO: Chrysostom Press, 2007.

_____. *The Explanation by Blessed Theophylact of the Holy Gospel According to Luke*. Trans. Fr Christopher Stade. House Springs, MO: Chrysostom Press, 1997.

_____. *The Explanation by Blessed Theophylact of the Holy Gospel According to St. Mark*. Trans. Fr Christopher Stade. House Springs, MO: Chrysostom Press, 1993.

_____. *The Explanation by Blessed Theophylact of the Holy Gospel According to St. Matthew*. Trans. Fr Christopher Stade. House Springs, MO: Chrysostom Press, 1993.

Vespers and Divine Liturgy of St Basil the Great for Great and Holy Saturday. Ed. Fr Paul Lazor. Latham, NY: Department of Religious Education, Orthodox Church in America, 1986.

Secondary Works Cited (*Theology and History*)

Arndt, William F. and Gingrich, F. W. *A Greek-English Lexicon of the New Testament and Other Early Christian Literature*. Chicago: University of Chicago Press, 1957.

Behr, John. *Becoming Human: Meditations on Christian Anthropology in Word and Image*. Crestwood, NY: St Vladimir's Seminary Press, 2013.

Harvey, S. A. "Embodiment in Time and Eternity: A Syriac Perspective." *St Vladimir's Theological Quarterly* 43 (1999): 125–26.

Hinshaw, Daniel B. *Suffering and the Nature of Healing*. Yonkers, NY: St Vladimir's Seminary Press, 2013.

Iftimiu, Aurelian. "Solemn and Commemorative Year 2017 officially proclaimed in the Romanian Patriarchate." News Agency Basilica.ro, January 3, 2017, accessed April 30, 2017. http://basilica.ro/en/solemn-and-commemorative-year-2017-officially-proclaimed-in-the-romanian-patriarchate/.

Keselopoulos, A. G. *Man and the Environment: A Study of St Symeon the New Theologian*. Trans. Elizabeth Theokritoff. Crestwood, NY: St Vladimir's Seminary Press, 2001.

Kushiner, J. M. "Solitary Refinement: How One Man Found Freedom Inside a Communist Prison; An Interview with Fr. Roman Braga," accessed April 26, 2017. http://www.salvomag.com/new/articles/salvo26/solitary-refinement.php.

Lewis, C. S. *The Four Loves*. London: Collins Fontana Books, 1974.

The Little Flowers of St Francis. Trans. Raphael Brown. Garden City, NY: Image Books, 1958.

Nyrop, Kristoffer. *The Kiss and Its History*. Trans. W. F. Harvey. New York: E. P. Dutton and Co., 1902.

Ouspensky, Leonid and Lossky, Vladimir. *The Meaning of Icons*. Trans. G. E. H. Palmer and E. Kadloubovsky. 2nd ed. Crestwood, NY: St Vladimir's Seminary Press, 1999.

Pascal, Blaise [1623–1662]. *Pascal's Penseés*. Trans. W. F. Trotter. New York: E. P. Dutton, 1958.

Shemunkasho, Aho. *Healing in the Theology of Saint Ephrem*. Piscataway, NJ: Gorgias Press, 2004.

Sherrard, Philip. *Christianity and Eros: Essays on the Theme of Sexual Love*. Limni, Evia, Greece: Denise Harvey Publisher, 1995.

Velimirović, (St) Nikolai. *The Prologue from Ochrid*, Vol. 3. Trans. Mother Maria. Birmingham, UK: Lazarica, 1986.

Secondary Works Cited (Medical and Scientific)

Bates, R. C.; Buret, A.; van Helden, E. F.; Horton, M. A.; and Burns, G. F. "Apoptosis Induced by Inhibition of Intercellular Contact," *Journal of Cell Biology* 125.2 (1994): 403–15.9

Clark, D. "'Total pain,' disciplinary power and the body in the work of Cicely Saunders, 1958–1967." *Social Science & Medicine* 49 (1999): 727–36.

Cox, J. J., et al. "An SCN9A Channelopathy Causes Congenital Inability to Experience Pain." *Nature* 444 (2006): 894–98.

Craig, A. D. "A new view of pain as a homeostatic emotion." *Trends in Neurosciences* 26.6 (2003): 303–7.

English, R. B. "Democritus' Theory of Sense Perception." *Transactions and Proceedings of the American Philological Association* 46 (1915): 217–27.

Field, T. "Enhancing Growth." In *Touch Therapy*. London: Churchill Livingstone, 2000.

Frisch, S. M. and Ruoslahti, E. "Integrins and Anoikis." *Current Opinion in Cell Biology* 9 (1997): 701–6.

Gardner, E. P. "Touch." Pp. 1–12. *Encyclopedia of Life Sciences*. Chichester, UK: John Wiley and Sons, May 2010.

Lam, D. K. et al. "TMPRSS2, a Novel Membrane-Anchored Mediator in Cancer Pain." *Pain* 156.5 (2015): 923–30.

McCabe, C.; Rolls, E. T.; Bilderbeck, A.; and McGlone, F. "Cognitive Influences on the Affective Representation of Touch and the Sight of Touch in the Human Brain." *Social Cognitive and Affective Neuroscience* 3 (2008): 97–108.

Mitchinson, A. M.; Kim, H. M.; Rosenberg, J. M.; Geisser, M.; Kirsh, M.; Cikrit, D.; and Hinshaw, D. B. "Acute Post-Operative Pain Management Using Massage as Adjuvant Therapy: A Randomized Trial." *Archives of Surgery* 142.12 (2007):1158–67.

Montagu, A. *Touching: The Human Significance of the Skin*, 3rd ed. New York: HarperCollins, 1986.

Nguyen, B. T., et al. "Face Representation in the Human Primary Somatosensory Cortex." *Neuroscience Research* 50 (2004): 227–32.

Penfield, W. and Boldrey, E. "Somatic Motor and Sensory Representation in the Cerebral Cortex of Man as Studied by Electrical Stimulation." *Brain Journal* 60 (1937): 389–443.

Retiefand, F. P. and Cilliers, L. "Christ's Crucifixion as a Medico-Historical Event." *Acta Theologica*, supp. 7, 26.2 (2006): 294–309.

Rolls, E. T. "The Affective and Cognitive Processing of Touch, Oral Texture, and Temperature in the Brain." *Neuroscience and Biobehavioral Reviews* 34 (2010): 237–45.

Thakur, S.; Dworkin, R. H.; Haroun, O. M. O.; Lockwood, D. N. J.; and Rice, A. S. C. "Acute and chronic pain associated with leprosy." *Pain* 156 (2015): 998–1002.